AF262829

WINTER'S SONG

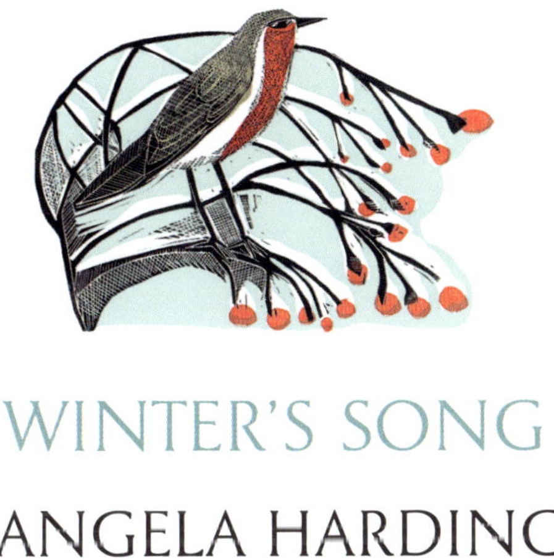

WINTER'S SONG

ANGELA HARDING

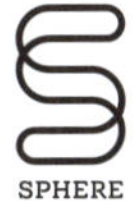

SPHERE

SPHERE

First published in Great Britain in 2025 by Sphere
3 5 7 9 10 8 6 4
Copyright © Angela Harding 2025

The moral right of the author has been asserted.

A CIP catalogue for this book is available from the British Library.

ISBN 9781408721964

Project Editor: Helen Brocklehurst
Production Manager: Abby Marshall
Cover and interior design: Ben Prior
Typeset in Spectral Light
Printed in Italy by Printer Trento Srl
Papers used by Sphere are from well-managed forests
and other responsible sources.

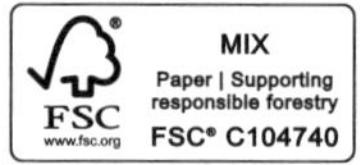

Sphere
An imprint of
Little, Brown Book Group
Carmelite House
50 Victoria Embankment
London EC4Y 0DZ

The authorised representative
in the EEA is
Hachette Ireland
8 Castlecourt Centre
Dublin 15, D15 XTP3, Ireland
(email: info@hbgi.ie)

An Hachette UK Company
www.hachette.co.uk
www.littlebrown.co.uk

For my husband, Mark Dyas

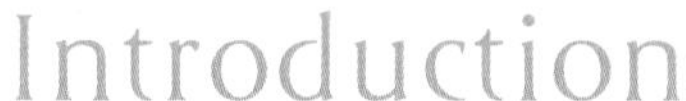

Introduction

Winter can be a difficult time for many people. The long, dark nights, the short days, the greyness and lack of sunlight. It is an even more difficult time for wildlife. Food becomes scarce and sharp, cold nights are difficult to survive. To help the birds, I leave my garden in rather a messy state, the summer growth of many plants left uncut and gone to seed. It may look untidy, but these seedheads become a valuable food source.

Tall teasels are just outside my sitting-room window, it is a great joy to see these topped with goldfinches. In the winter months, we have a daily flock of finches that visit. They balance on the seedheads like acrobats, dressed in smart red, yellow, black and white suits. They hang upside down, bending the teasel heads over so they can get every seed. The goldfinches prefer the teasel seeds to the bountiful supply of bird food I put out for them and the other garden birds. The teasels are now well established in my garden, and I will continue to grow them, if only for the joy of watching goldfinches feeding.

Snow days have always been very inspiring for my work. When it snows, I am a child again. I must go out for a crunching, snowy walk and experience the landscape transformed. It is a cliche to call it Narnia, but when the snow falls thickly, it does bring dramatic change that makes our familiar village feel like a new place, a place unknown. Hare, rabbit and bird tracks become visible in the lanes and fields. The world is quiet and still. Birds no longer sing, except for the robin; the robin song becomes voluminous. This small bird puffs up his red breast, the song notes tumble into the frosty air, the steam of his breath visible against the hedgerow. I can never get over the thinness of a robin's legs – how do they manage in that cold, in that snow,

Opposite:
Blackbird and Berries
(Linocut and silkscreen)

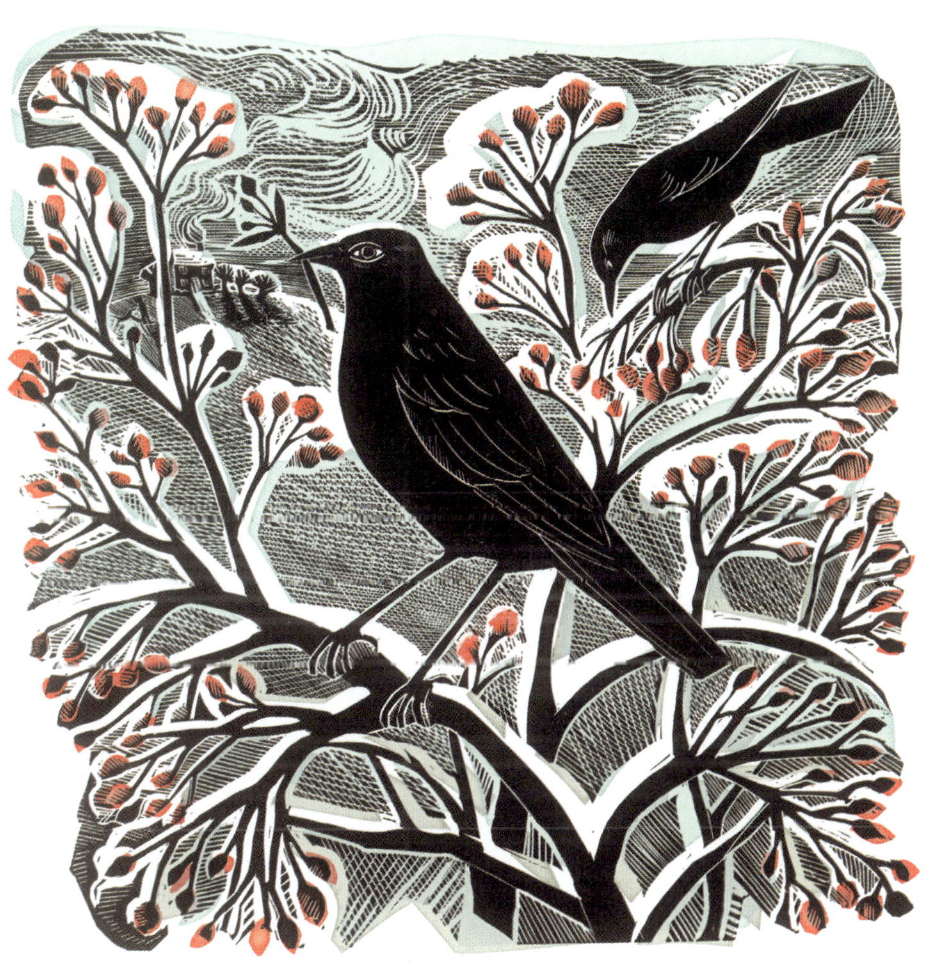

with those tiny, spindly legs? The robin
grips hard to the hawthorn hedge, perched
carefully between its thorns, and sings and
sings and sings.

But snowy days are rare; more common
are many days of rain, and mud – lots of
mud. These grey, muddy days can be a
little depressing. But as each day passes
to the next, we are just that bit nearer
to spring. When the year turns from
Christmas to January, little spots of white
appear in the brown, muddy soil. These
are the start of snowdrops; they begin to
appear in patches of greenish white. They
signal that, even in winter, nature's force
is there, pushing new growth through the
soil. These first flowers mean we will soon
see aconites and crocus, that winter will
be gone, and a new year will begin.

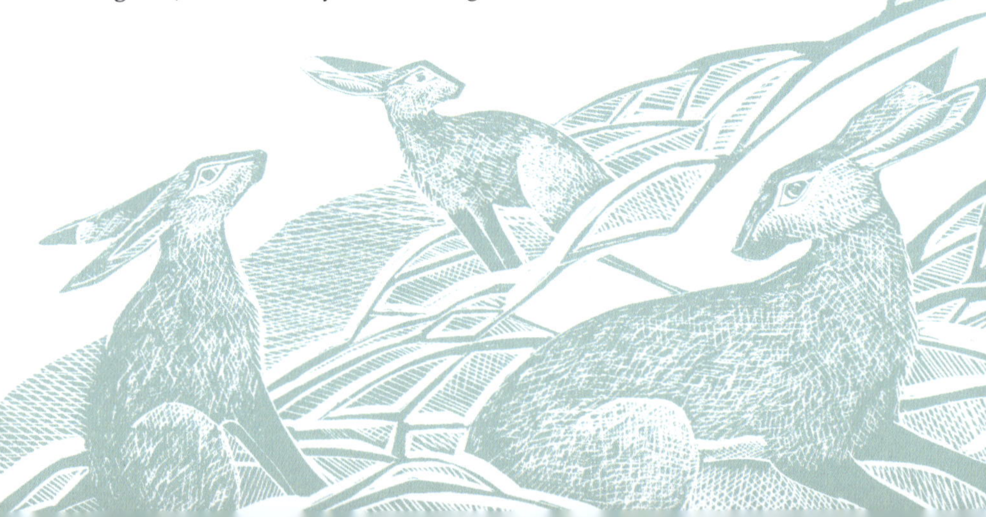

Winter's Song is the last in a series of four books that reflect on the seasons. This quartet has its origins in my first book, *A Year Unfolding*, which is a printmaker's view of the changing seasons. In *Winter's Song*, I have added new images and text to my original thoughts about winter. This book is a new format; a small book that you can put in your pocket to muse over on travels and in quiet moments, or a gift book to cherish with others who share my love of nature. The other books in this series are *Spring Unfurled*, *Summer's Hum* and *Falling into Autumn*.

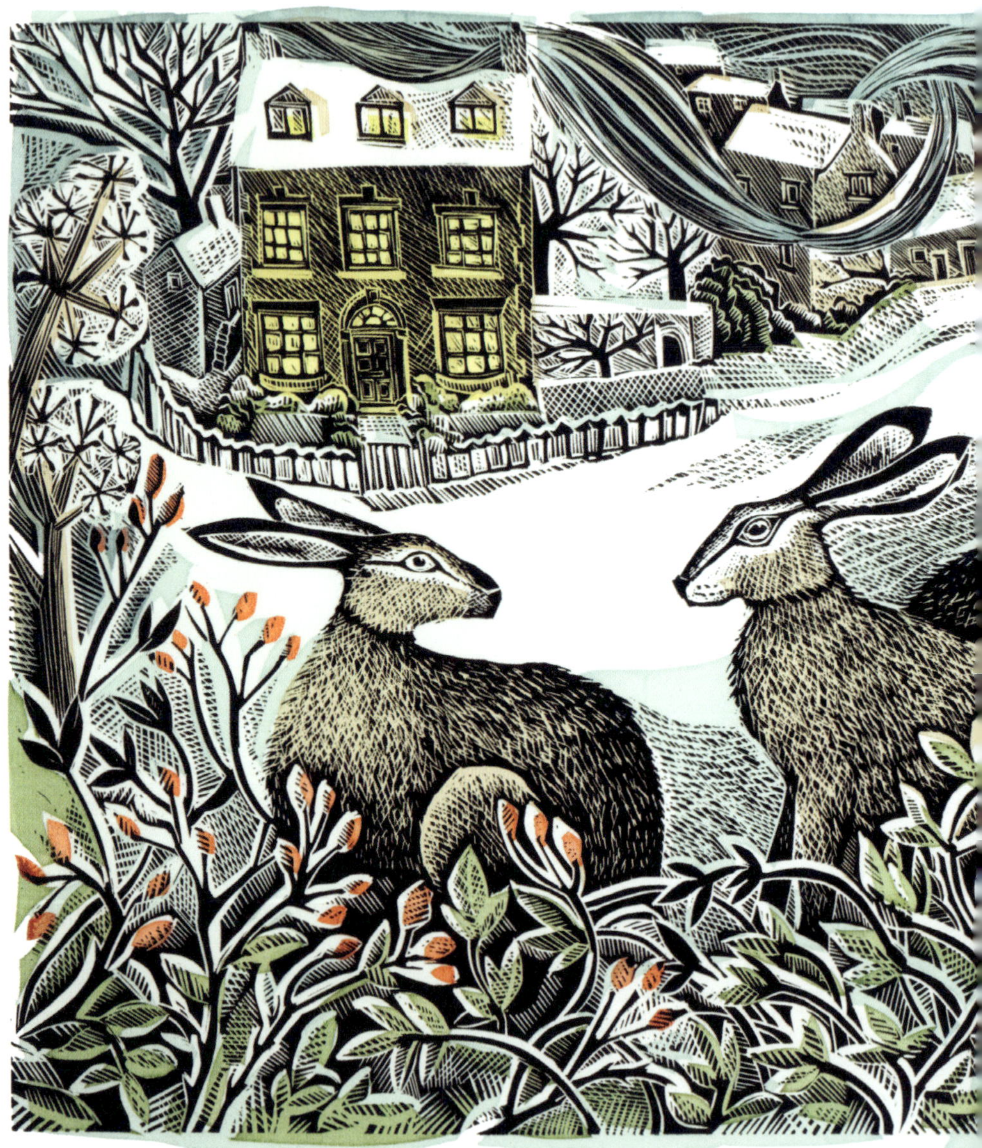

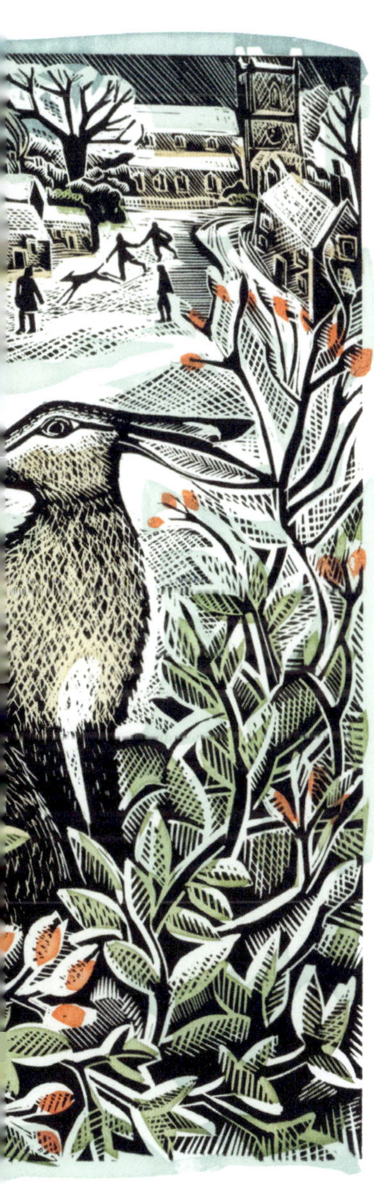

When winter days become shorter and shorter, a break in grey clouded skies is something that really lifts the spirits.

Opposite:
We Three Hares
(Linocut and silkscreen)

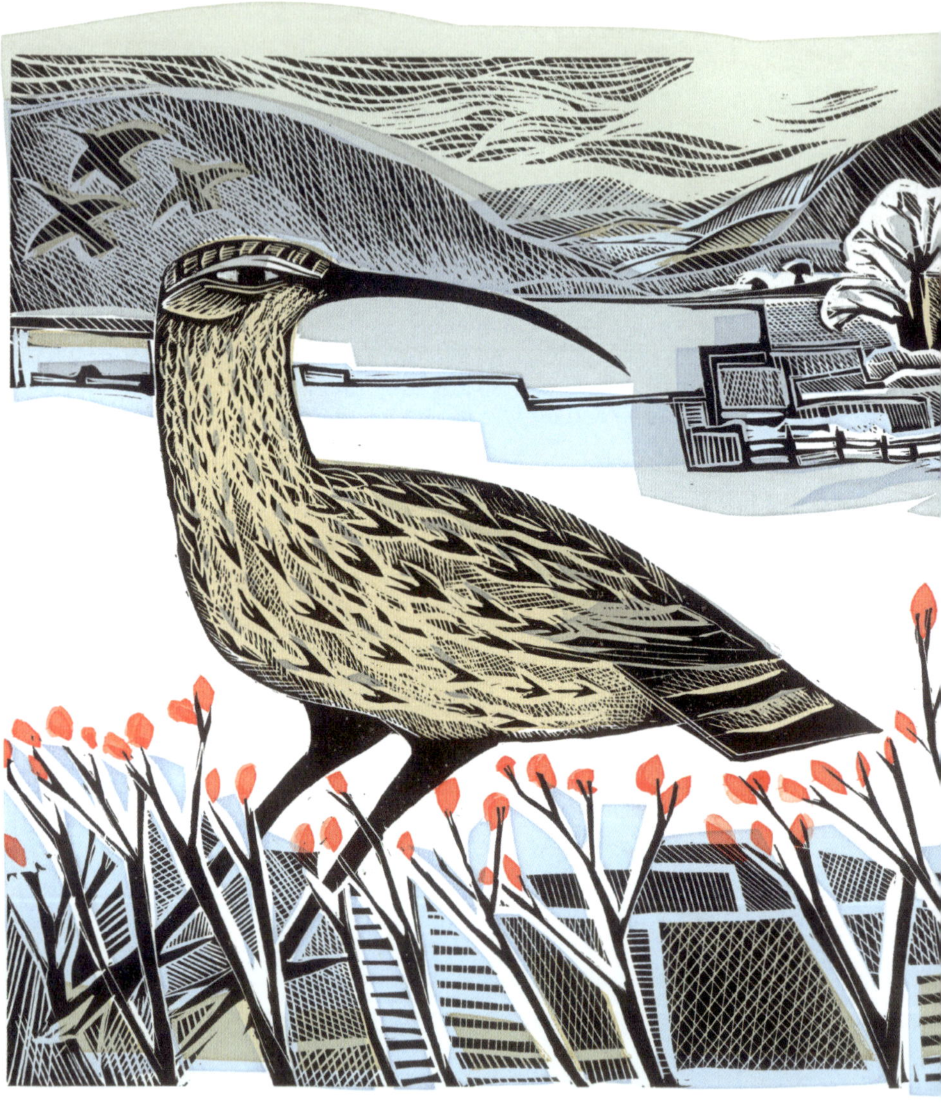

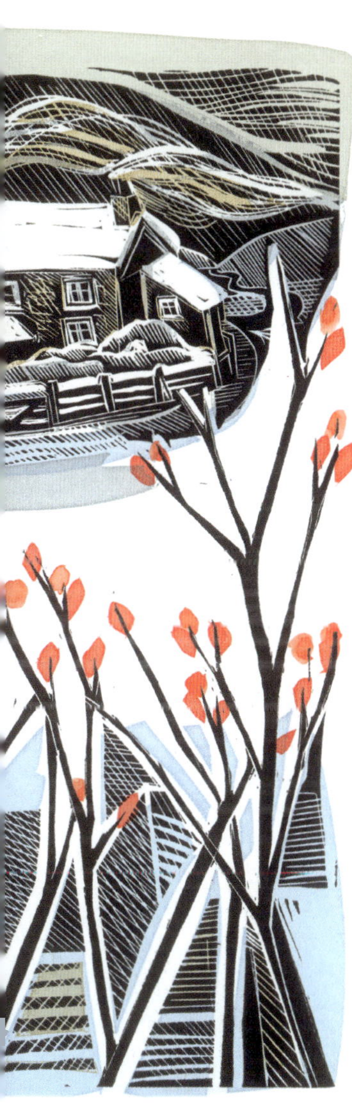

Thick snow in Wing is rare – in the sixteen years we have lived here, it has only happened three times – but in 2020 we had one of those snowfalls that in the course of one afternoon turned Wing into a place of true magic. As the snow falls, I am instantly turned back into a child and there is no point in trying to work – I want to be in that snow. It is never with us for long, so every moment is to be enjoyed. In my winter prints, I hope I convey the sense of excitement that the snow gives me.

Opposite:
Curlew in the Snow
(Linocut and
silkscreen)

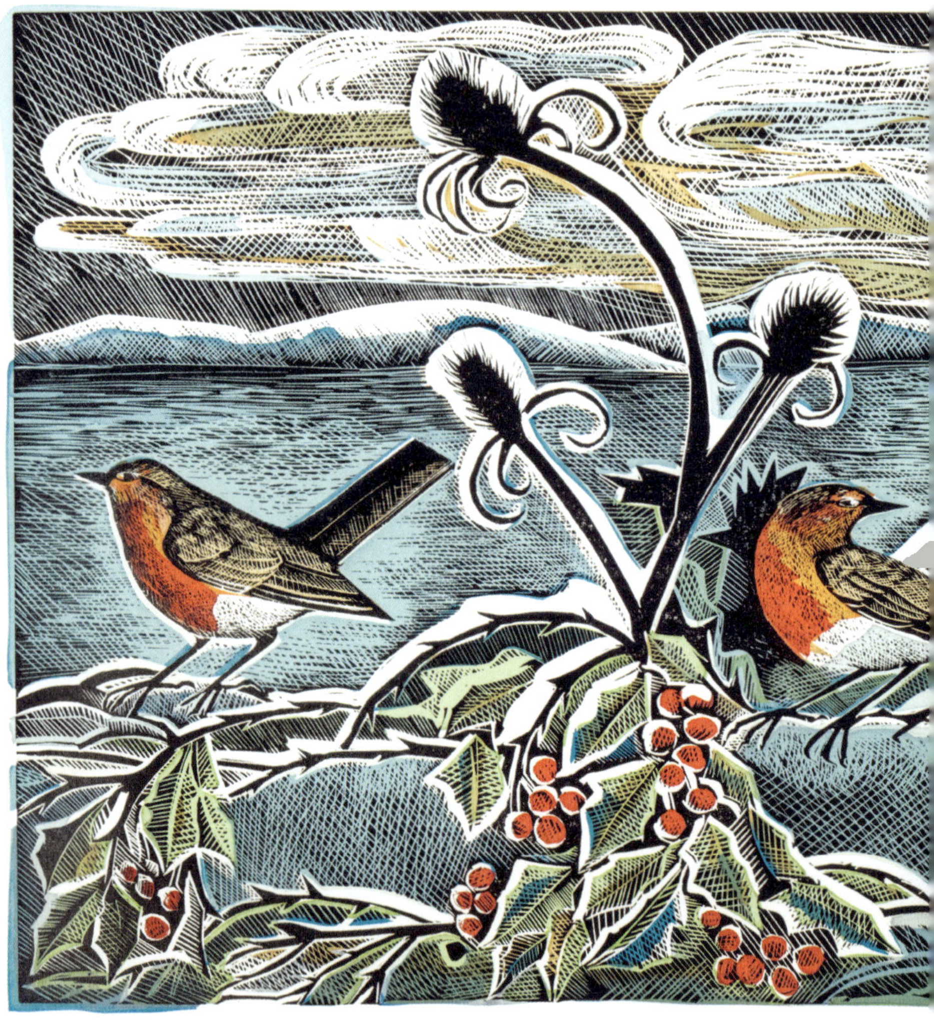

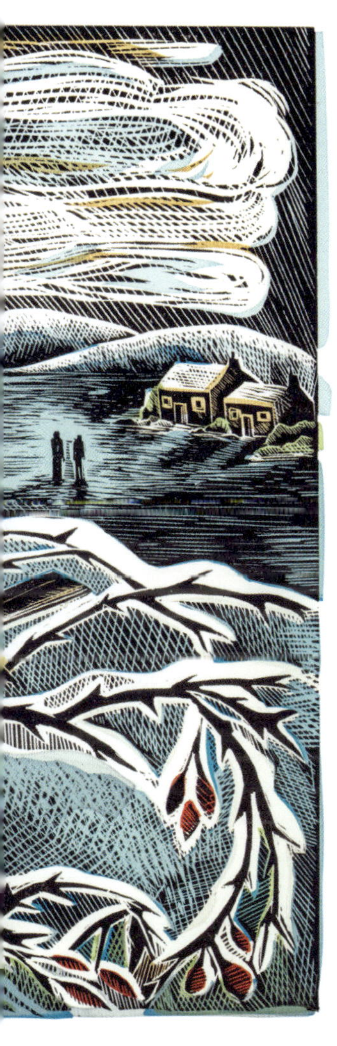

In winter: the ever-present song of robins and the deep caw-caw of rookeries – these sounds, along with lengthening shadows, are the signals that the day is almost finished.

Opposite:
Scottish Robins
(Linocut and
silkscreen)

I find winter images inspiring to create, the tree branches against the sky, and reducing colour use to a simpler palette suits the way I like to work.

Opposite:
Stopping by the Woods
(Linocut and silkscreen)

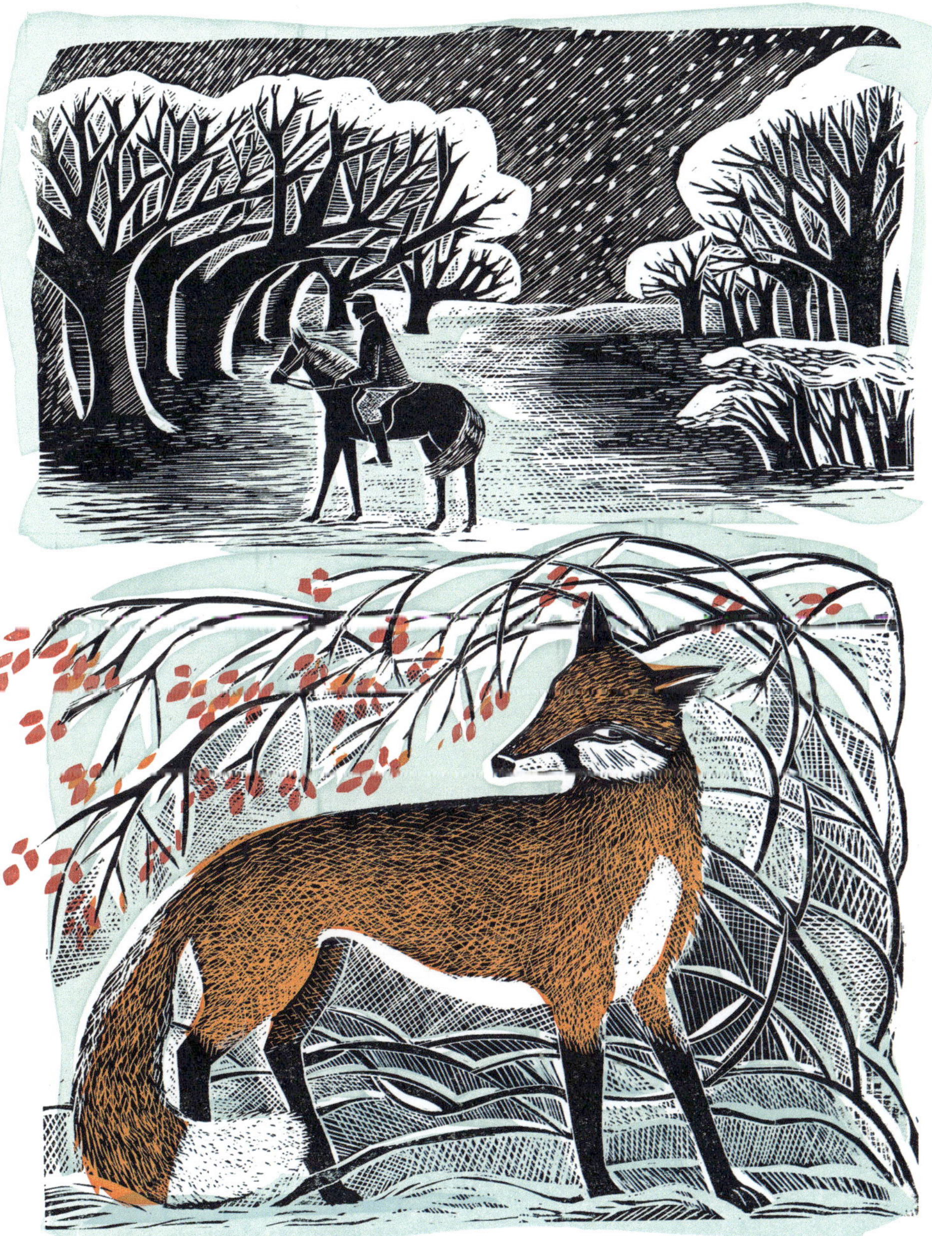

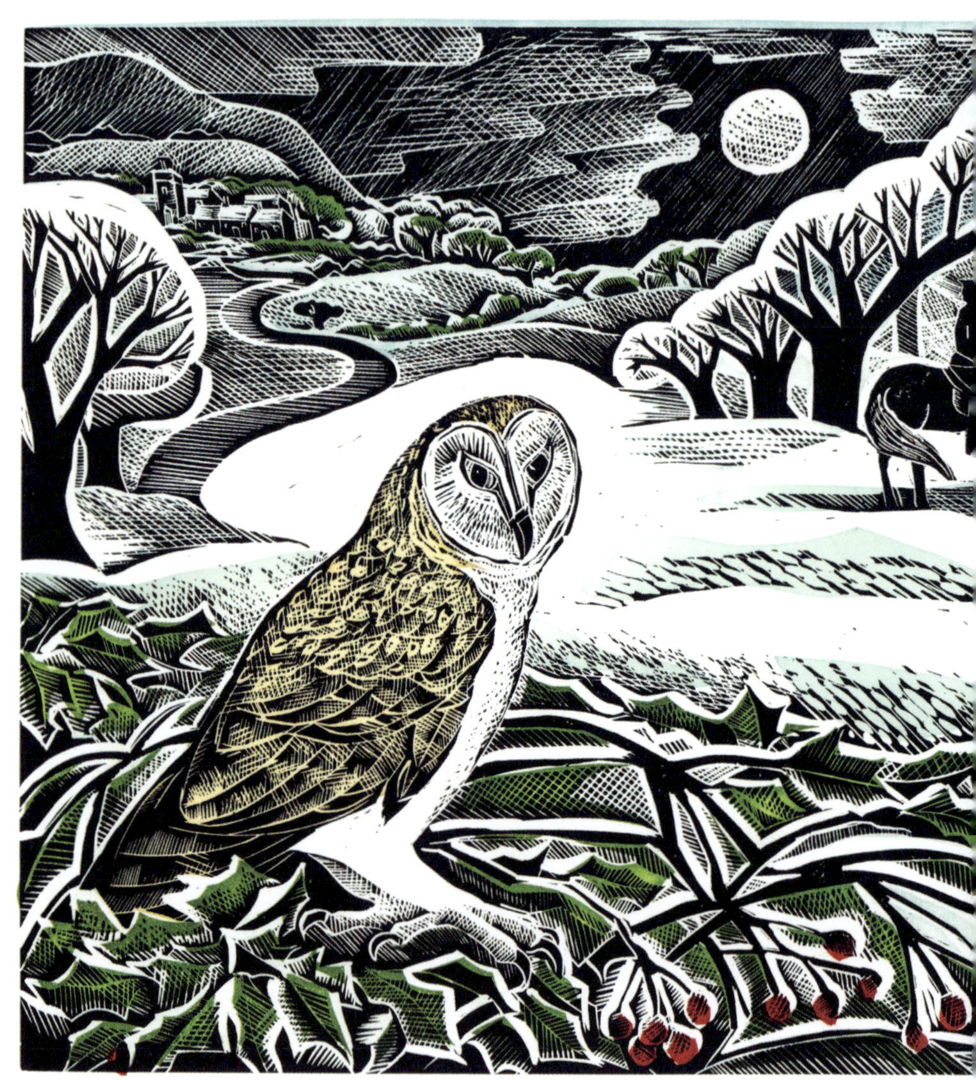

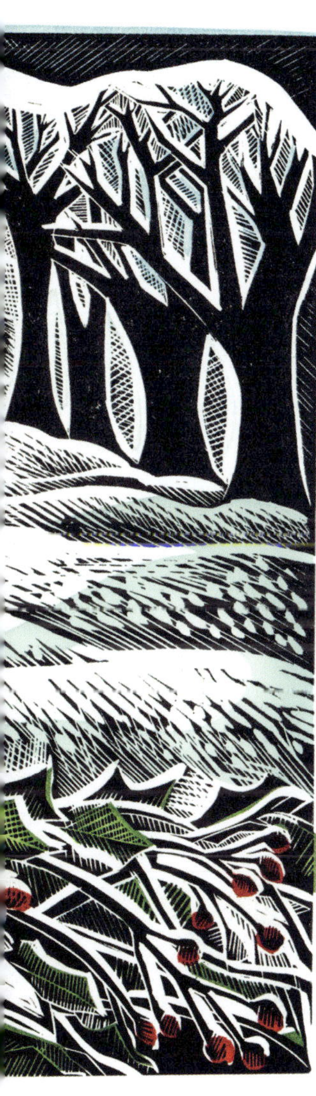

I revisited Robert Frost's beautiful poem 'Stopping by Woods on a Snowy Evening' for this image, which I hope evokes something of the mood of that poem. Seeing nature at night-time can be particularly rewarding, perhaps because it feels unusual; it is when the world is quiet, and it is often a solitary experience. Nature seeks time away from humans and night-time is its best opportunity for this. Nocturnal animals materialise in the time of day that makes for happy hunting. Hooting owls mark out their territory; snuffling badgers emerge from their setts.

Opposite:
Winter Wood
(Linocut and silkscreen)

This print is based on my father's house. He died in 2019 at the age of ninety-four, but he lived for more than forty years in the same cottage on the border of Wales in Shropshire. It was an iconic gingerbread cottage perched on the top of a crossroads that looked into Wales on one side and then out across the Shropshire plain on the other. It was the most amazing view and, according to my father, it gave him a view of more than half the width of the UK – which meant he could keep an eye on us wherever we were. To the back of the cottage is Bromlow Callow – a callow is a hill topped with a circle of distinctive trees. This is an image that often appears in my prints – that and his ever-present whippets.

Opposite:
Hope Park Cottage
(Linocut and
silkscreen)

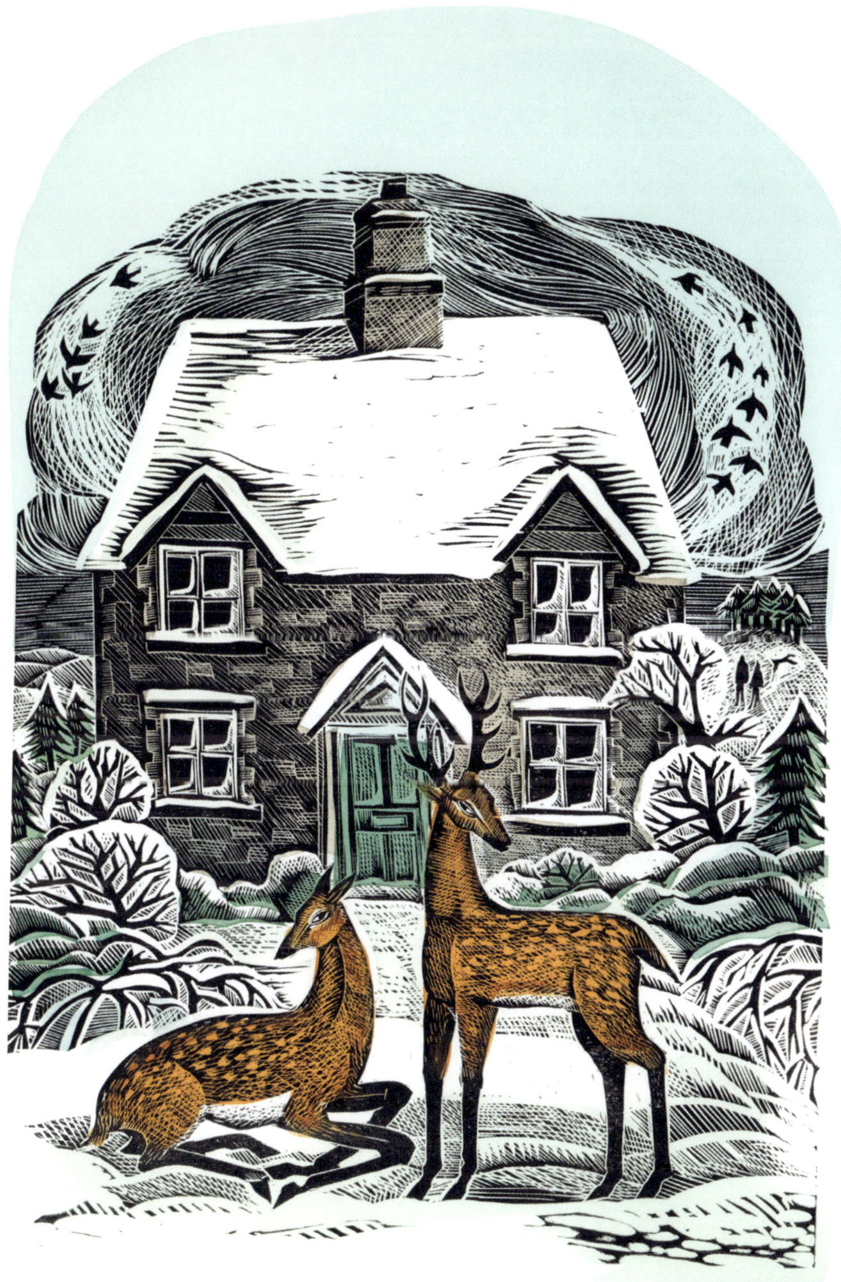

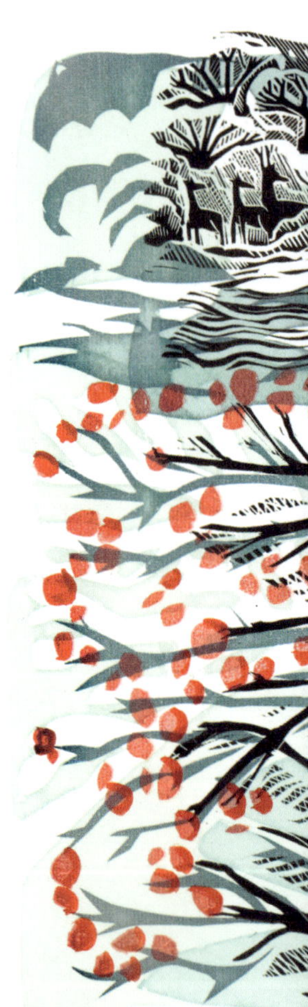

I have only been to the Scilly Isles once, in the winter of 2016. Tresco is famous for its gardens and in 2013 twenty red squirrels were introduced from the mainland in an experiment to see if they would settle and breed there. It has been a great success story: they have thrived, increasing their numbers to over a hundred. In February, there were only a few other visitors at the garden. Within minutes, we spotted two ginger dots, which turned out to be two red squirrels feeding close to the gate where we had just entered. We watched them, entranced, not daring to move, but then, as quickly as they had appeared they, were gone.

Opposite:
A Winter's Tale
(Linocut and silkscreen)

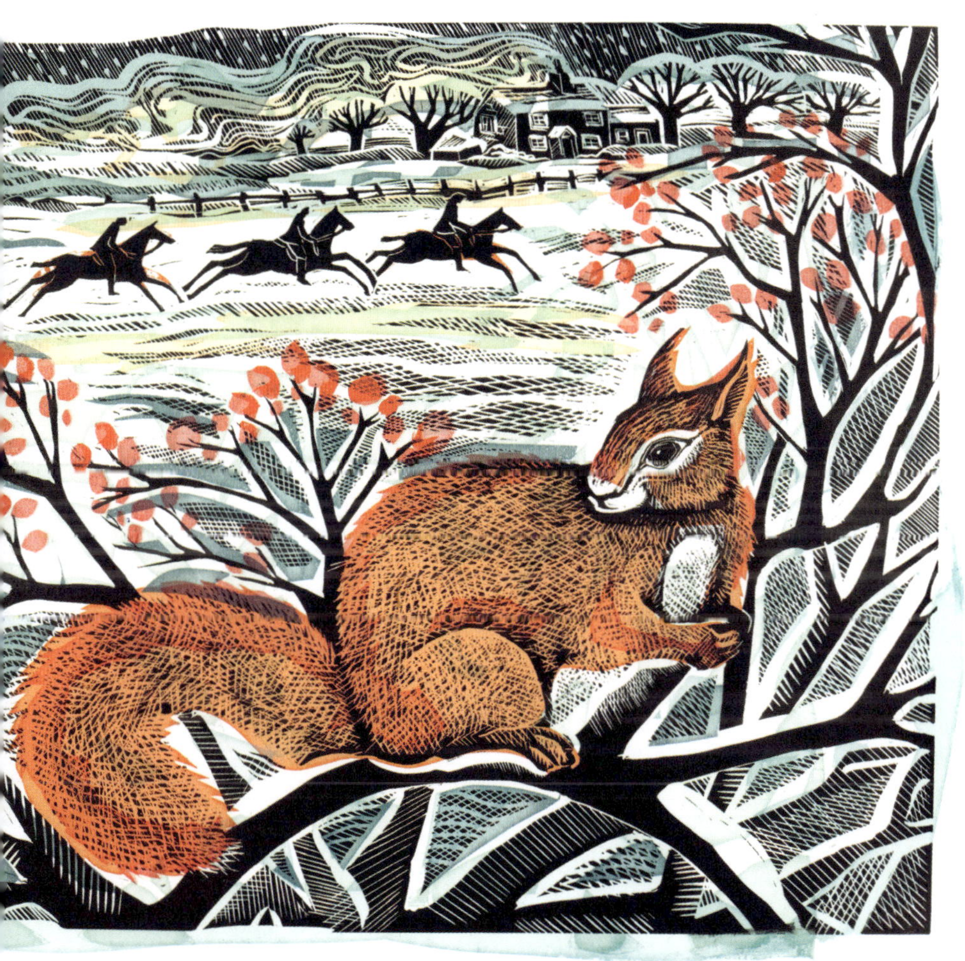

Our dogs have been a mixture of whippets and other sighthounds. They continue to act as models for my work and companions for my days and nights.

Opposite:
Whippet Wonderland
(Linocut and
silkscreen)

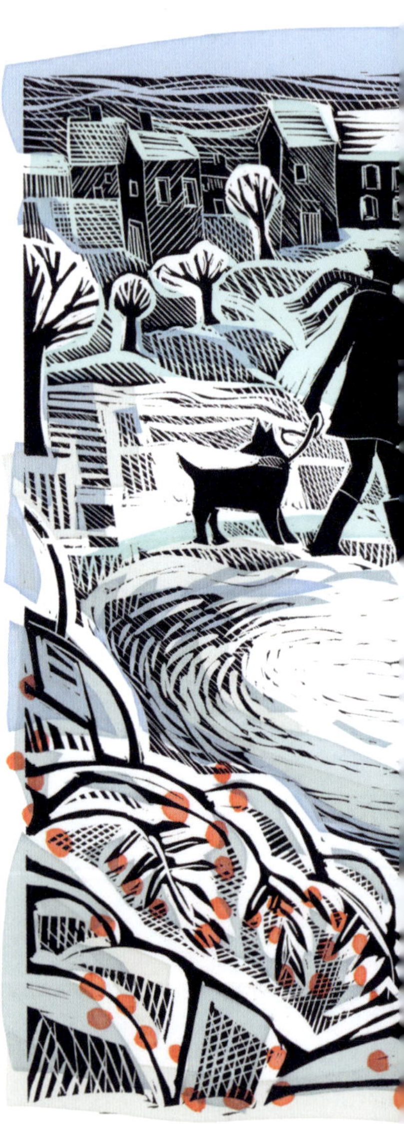

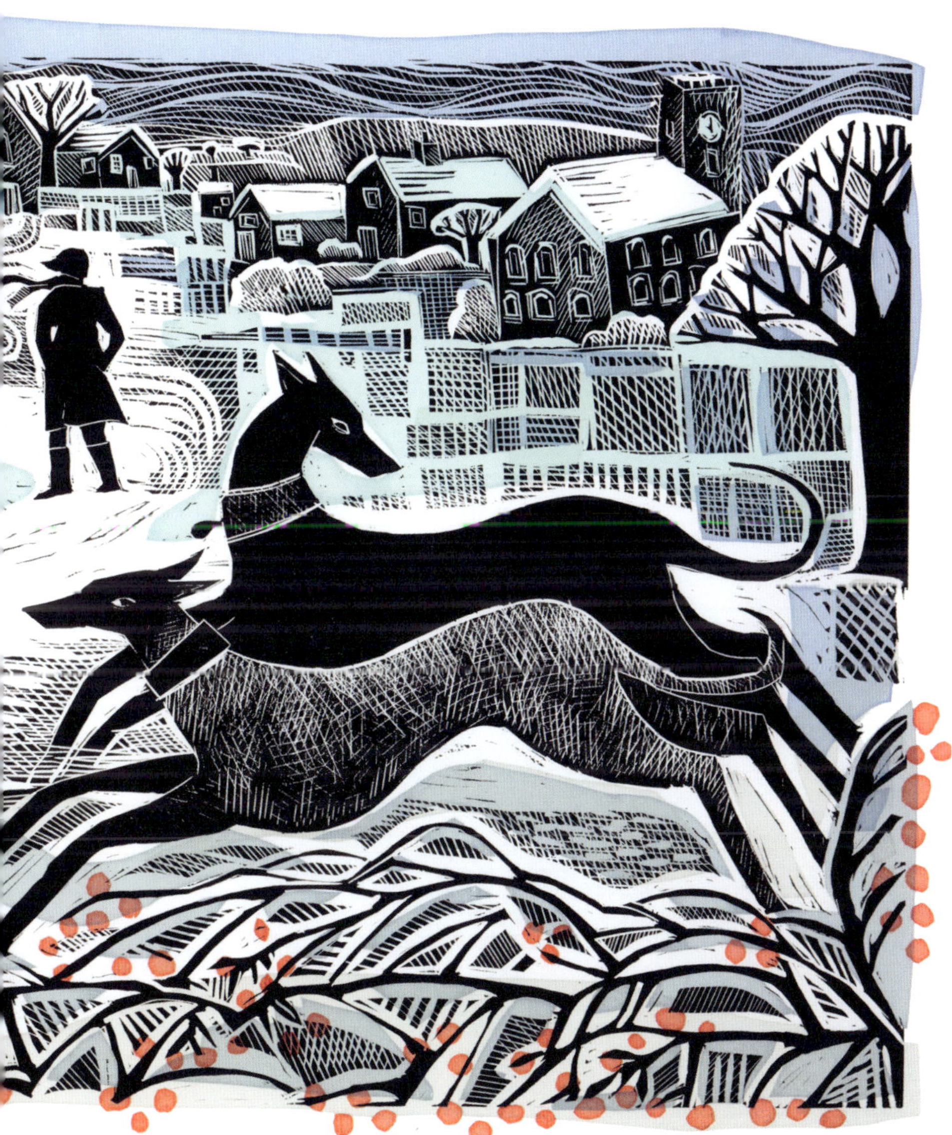

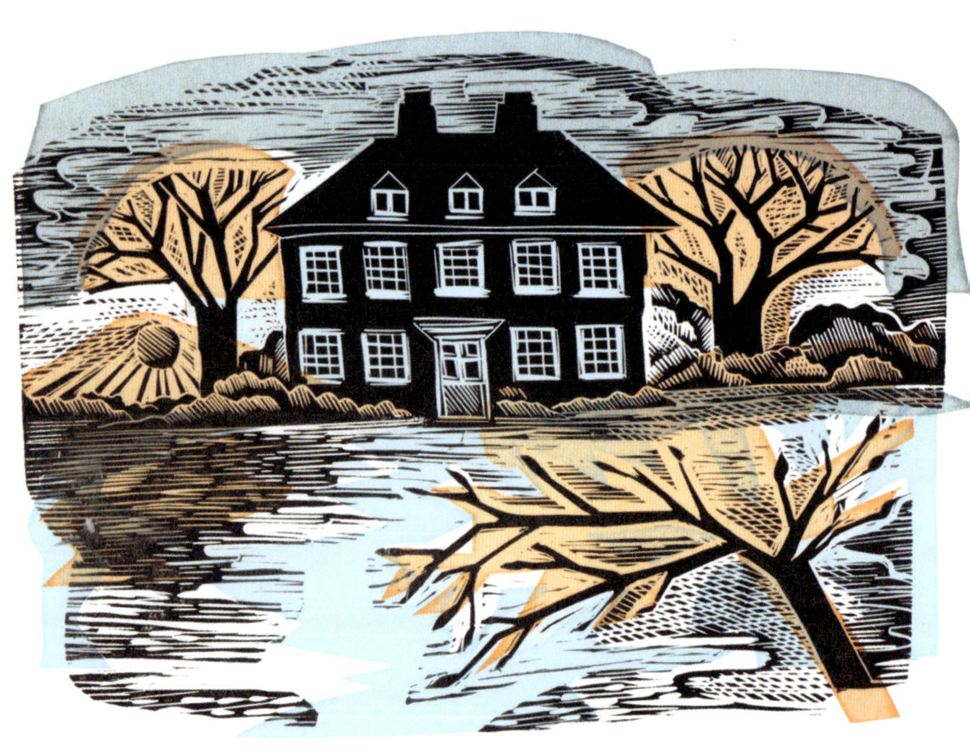

This image was commissioned by Penguin Books for the paperback version of *Sleep No More* by P. D. James. I created the hardback version the previous year, but for the paperback I endeavoured to give this image a still, cold and broodingly ominous atmosphere. I hope that it reflects both the story and the feel of winter.

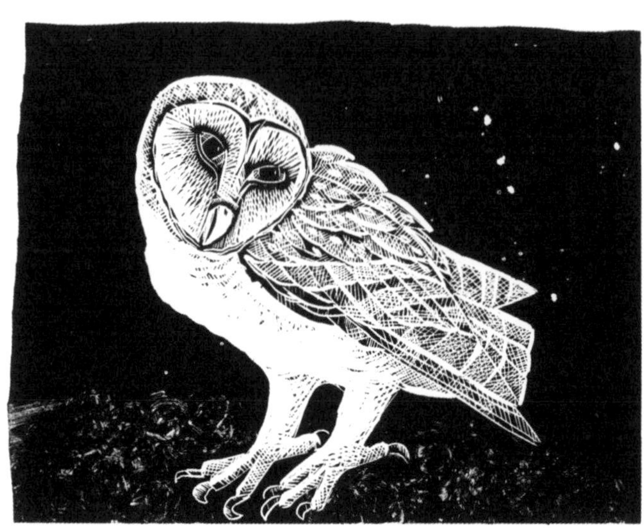

Owl Sequence
(Linocut)

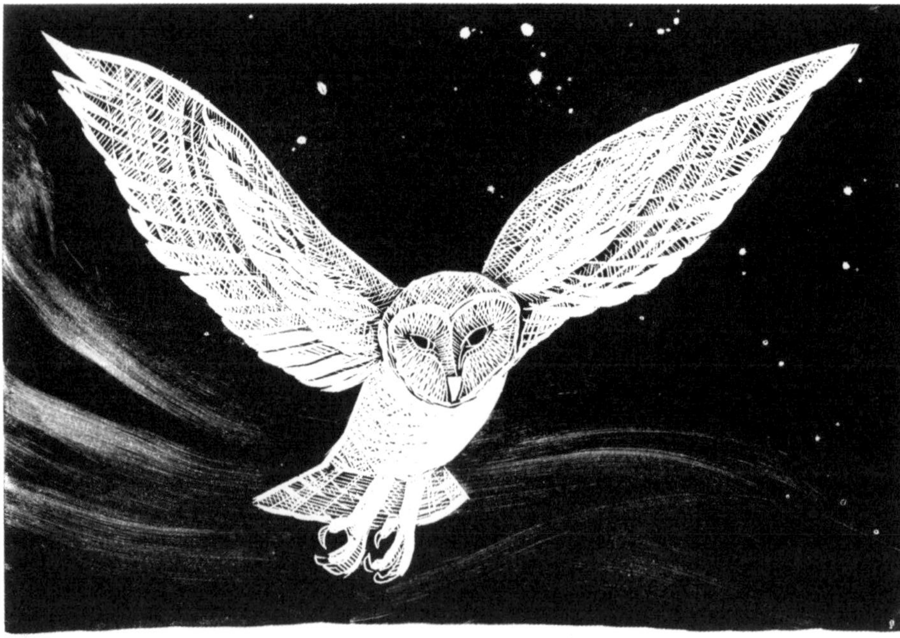

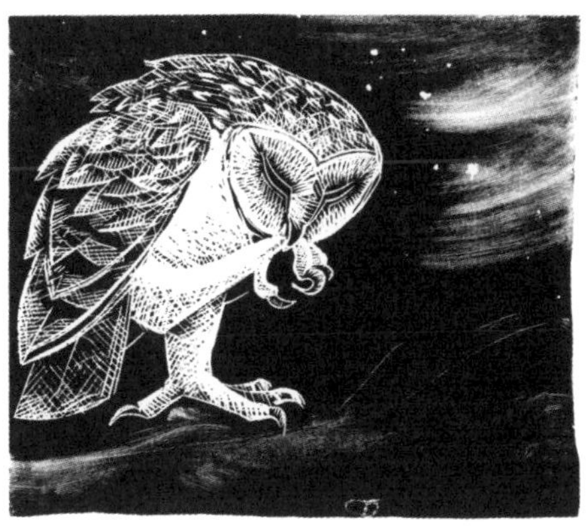

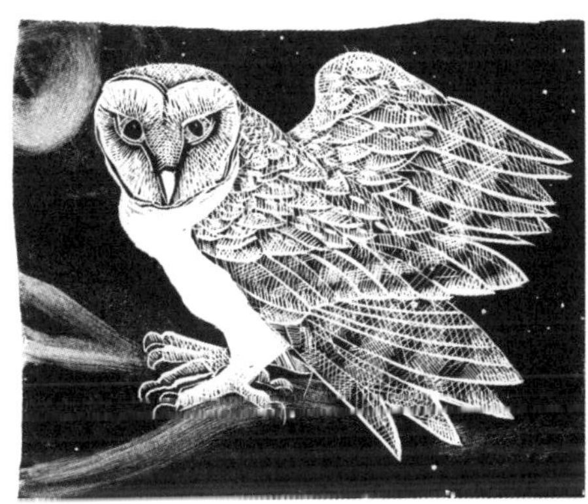

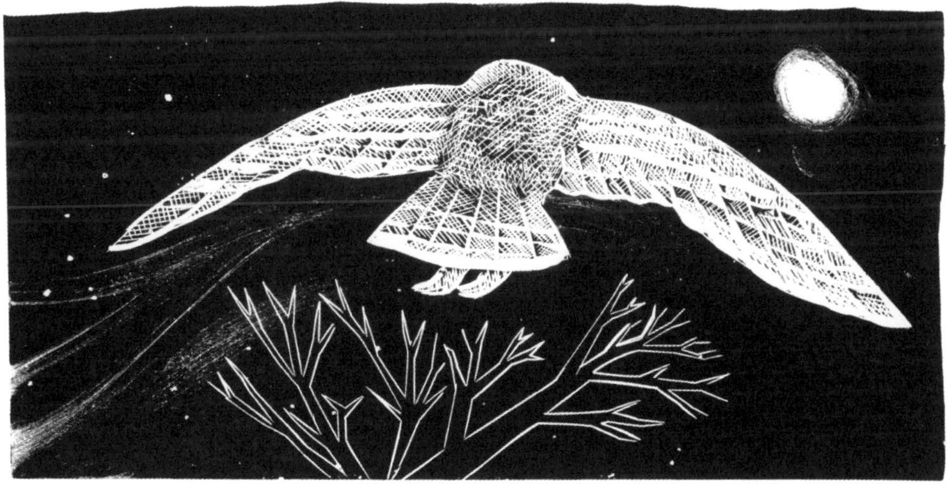

Being an illustrator can throw up some
interesting work; different briefs have
taken me in many different directions.
For over five years, I supplied a monthly
print for *Gardens Illustrated* magazine
to sit with a regular column about
gardening problems. The illustration
shown here accompanied one of these
articles. It was about gardening in very
cold climates and the importance of
good drainage. There is a large amount
of artistic licence used here, but I hope
the feeling of the illustration is of a
sharp, cold morning in cool, frosty light.

Opposite:
East Winds
(Linocut and
silkscreen)

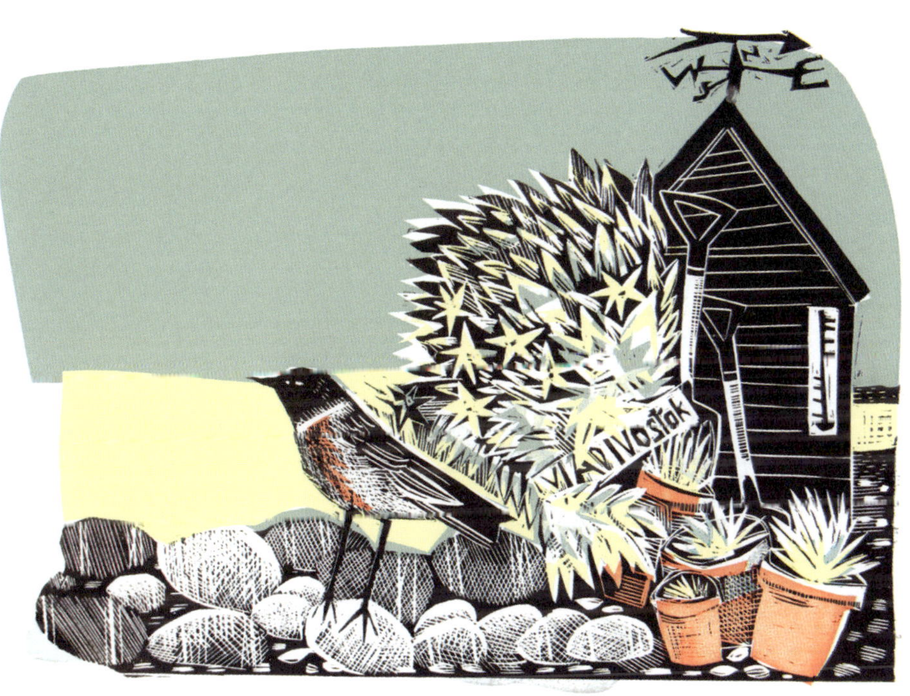

N
W   E
S
Vlad Ivostok

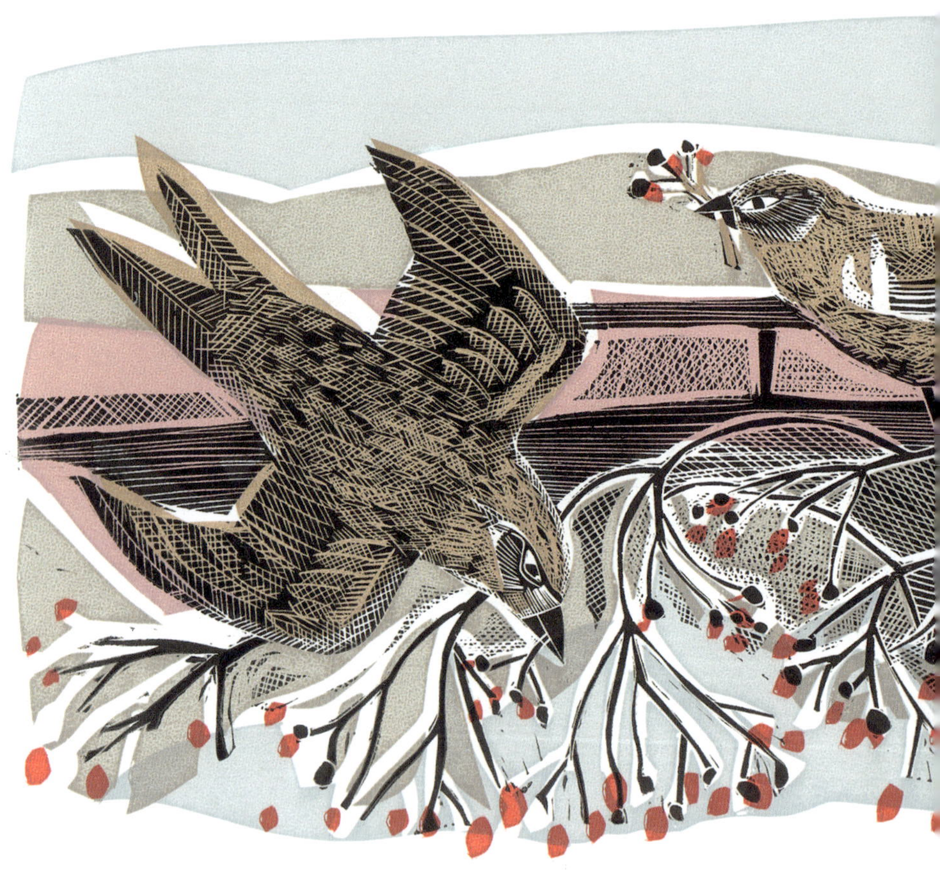

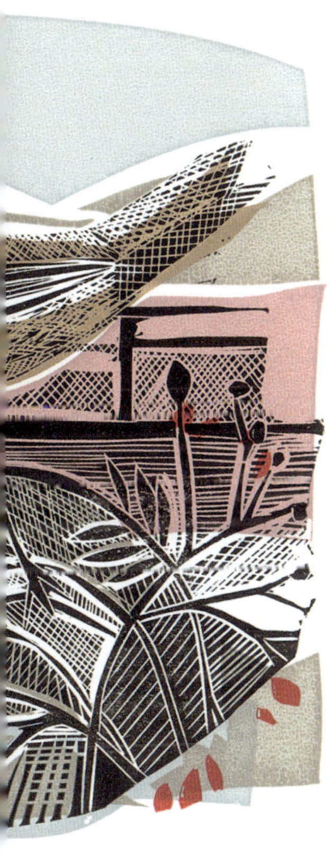

The fading light of winter is spent at home in Wing. After a day in my studio, it is a short walk up the garden path to home.

I love Christmas; as a family, we love all aspects of it, and though my family is now grown up, they all seem to have inherited this love of the festive period. Bringing home the tree is always special. Before I learned to drive at the age of thirty, I cycled everywhere – shopping, work and holidays. Bringing home a Christmas tree on a bike was no mean feat as it meant you had to strap it to the bike and literally ride it home. I wish I had a photo of that – but sadly not!

Opposite:
Bringing Back the Tree
(Linocut and silkscreen)

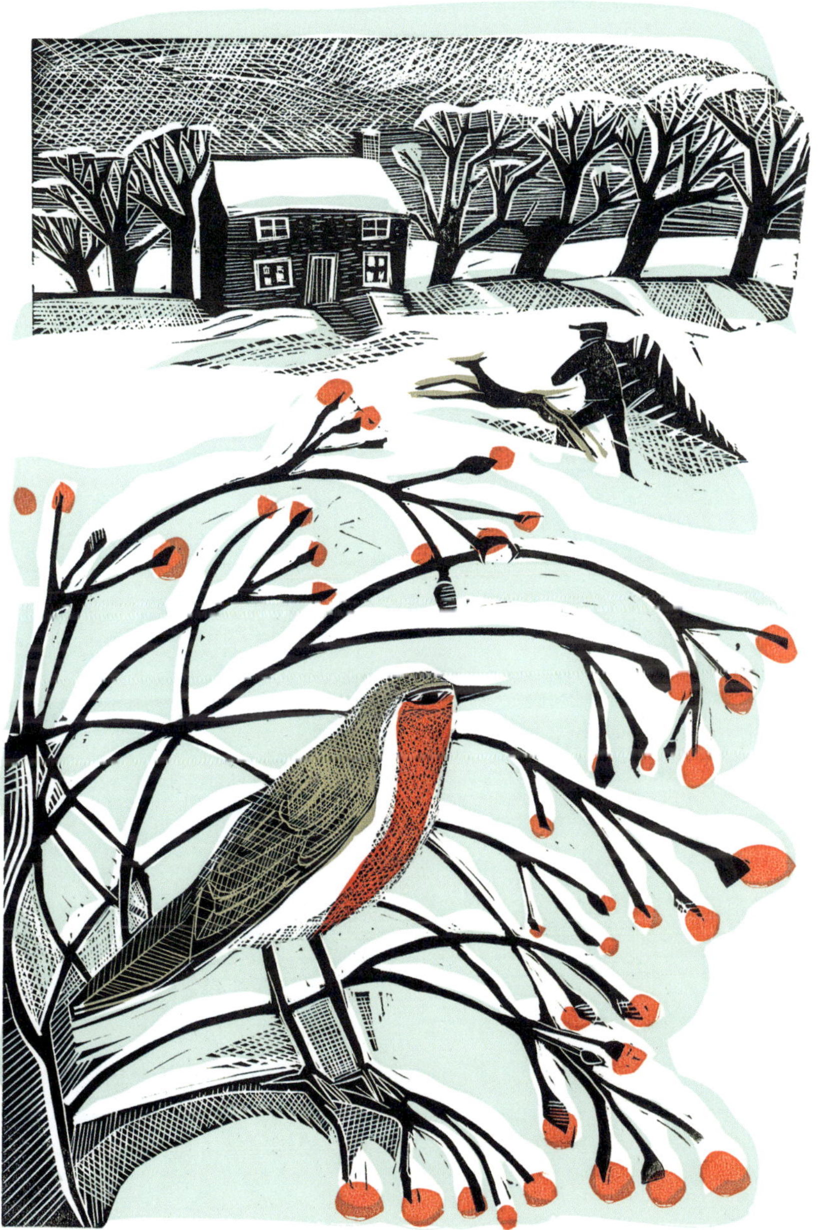

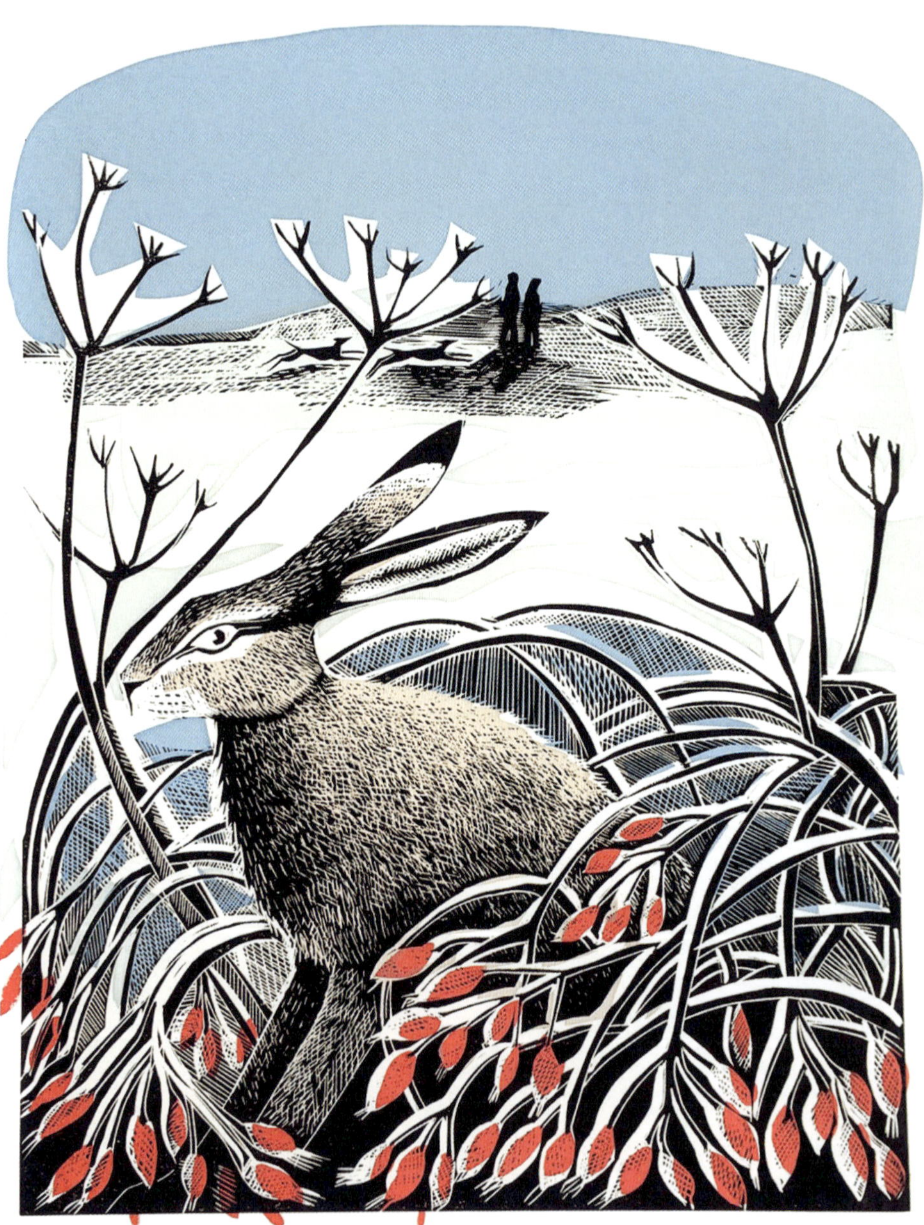

In *Winter Hare,* you can see Mark and me trudging through the snow watched by a wiry hare. This print is not accurate because, in truth, even when they were young, our two whippets would not go out in the cold without a coat. So, the bounding, coat-free sighthounds in the background is a bit of artistic licence. Though, a few years back, we did own a lurcher called Syd who was much hardier, and he loved the snow as much as we did.

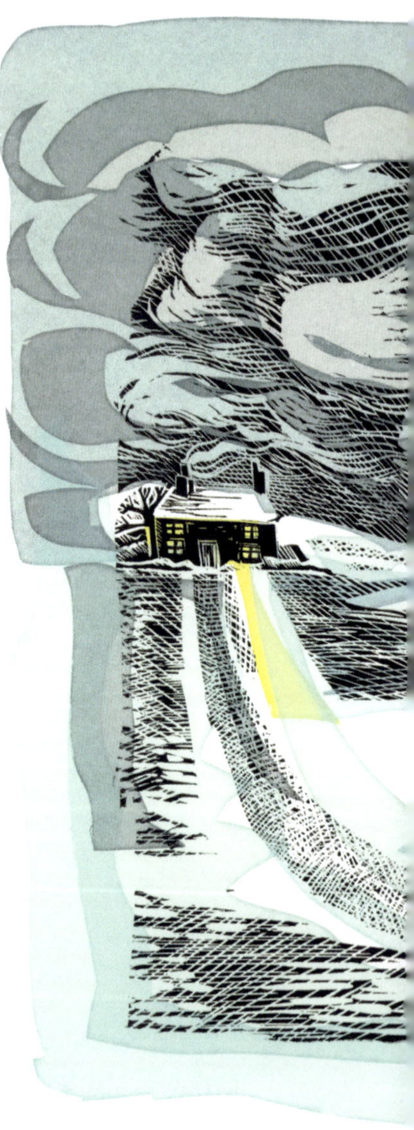

One of the aspects of my work that
has evolved over the years is making
an annual advent calendar – the ones
I create are, of course, just pictures,
but they seem to be enjoyed as much
by adults as by children. The images
are imagined, but I do add one or two
aspects from my home life.

Opposite:
Winter Fox
(Linocut and
silkscreen)

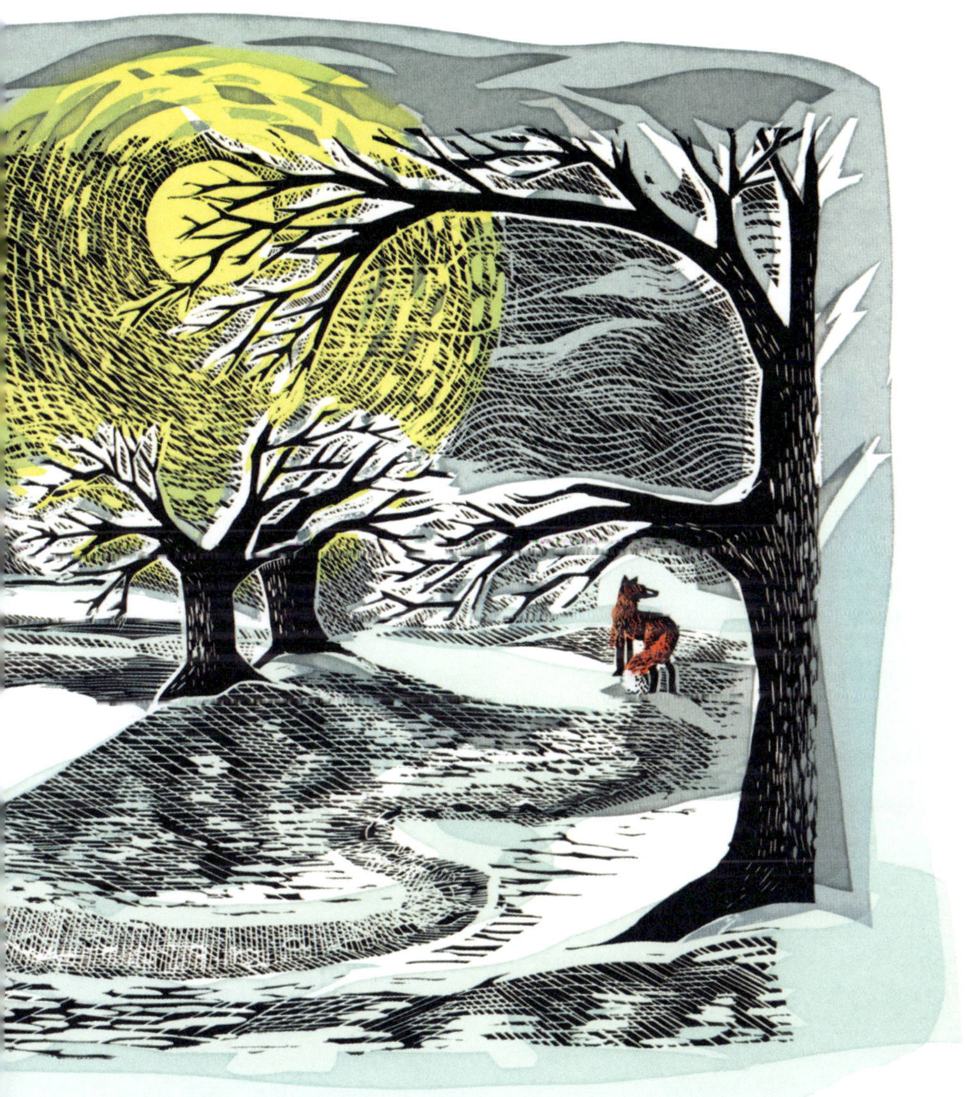

The hedgerows in winter are particularly beautiful, but they are also of great importance. They give shelter to our native birds that stay throughout the winter rather than migrate. In winter, there is a distinctive medley of calls that marks out a gang of blue, great, marsh, coal and long-tailed tits that have clubbed together to feed. The long-tailed tits are often in the garden on the bird feeder outside my studio windows. They really enjoy the fat balls and it is very important that these tiny birds take on enough calories to get them through the cold nights. Overnight, long-tailed tits will bed down together to conserve their energy. A thick shrub such as hawthorn is favoured, and individuals will huddle into a ball with their tails sticking out.

Opposite:
Holly Hedge
(Linocut and silkscreen)

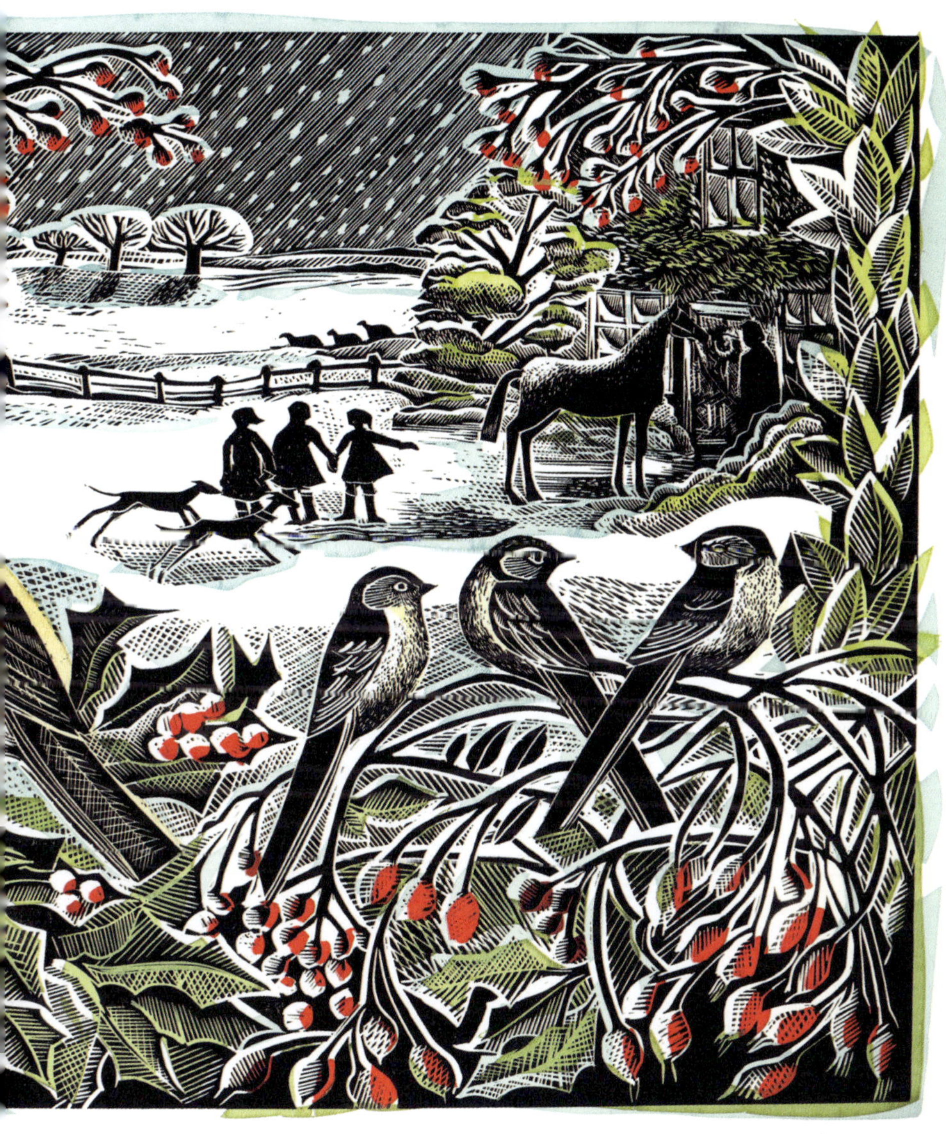

There is a good population of hares in our area; we see them all year round, but a snow-covered field really does give you an insight into their behaviour. Walking through the fields after a heavy snowfall, it is easy to spot hare tracks. The tracks are very distinctive due to the hares' large back feet and small front paws; they make the most beautiful criss-cross designs in the snow. If you are lucky, you can follow a track to see the silhouette of a hare against a bright white field.

Opposite:
Hares in Conversation
(Linocut and silkscreen)

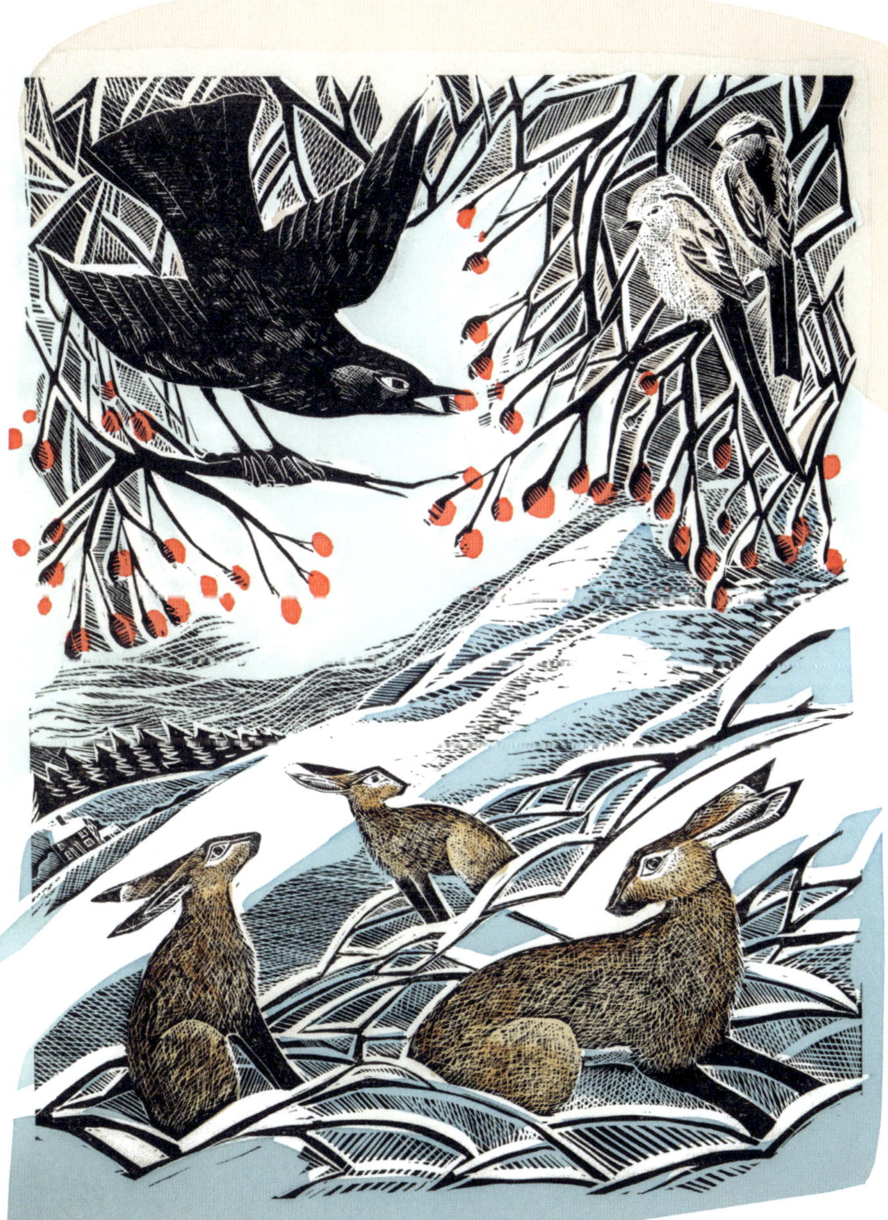

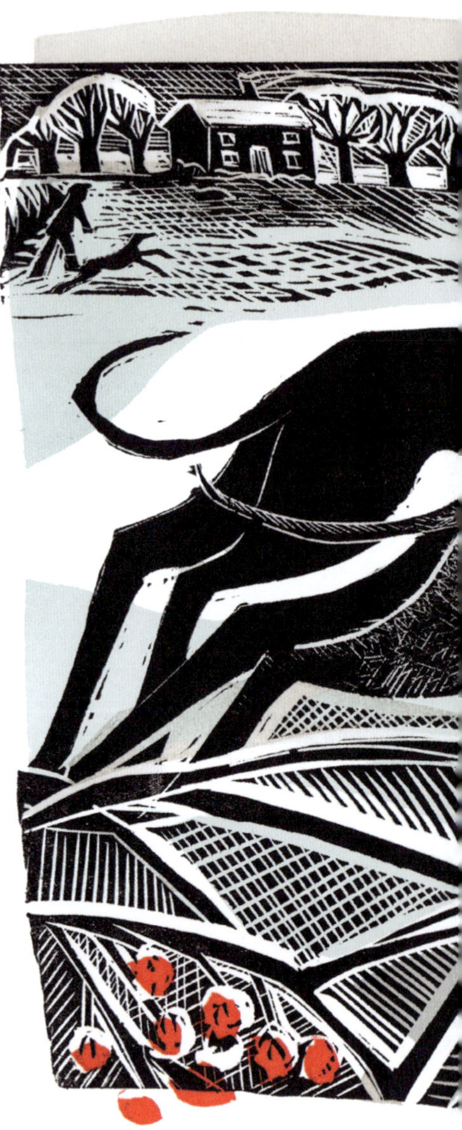

One of the great pleasures of owning sighthounds is seeing them run, but add in a snowy field and you will see the meaning of joy. Our whippets have always loved snow. It brings a new level of excitement that makes them jump, twirl and bounce with pleasure.

Opposite:
Evening Run
(Linocut and silkscreen)

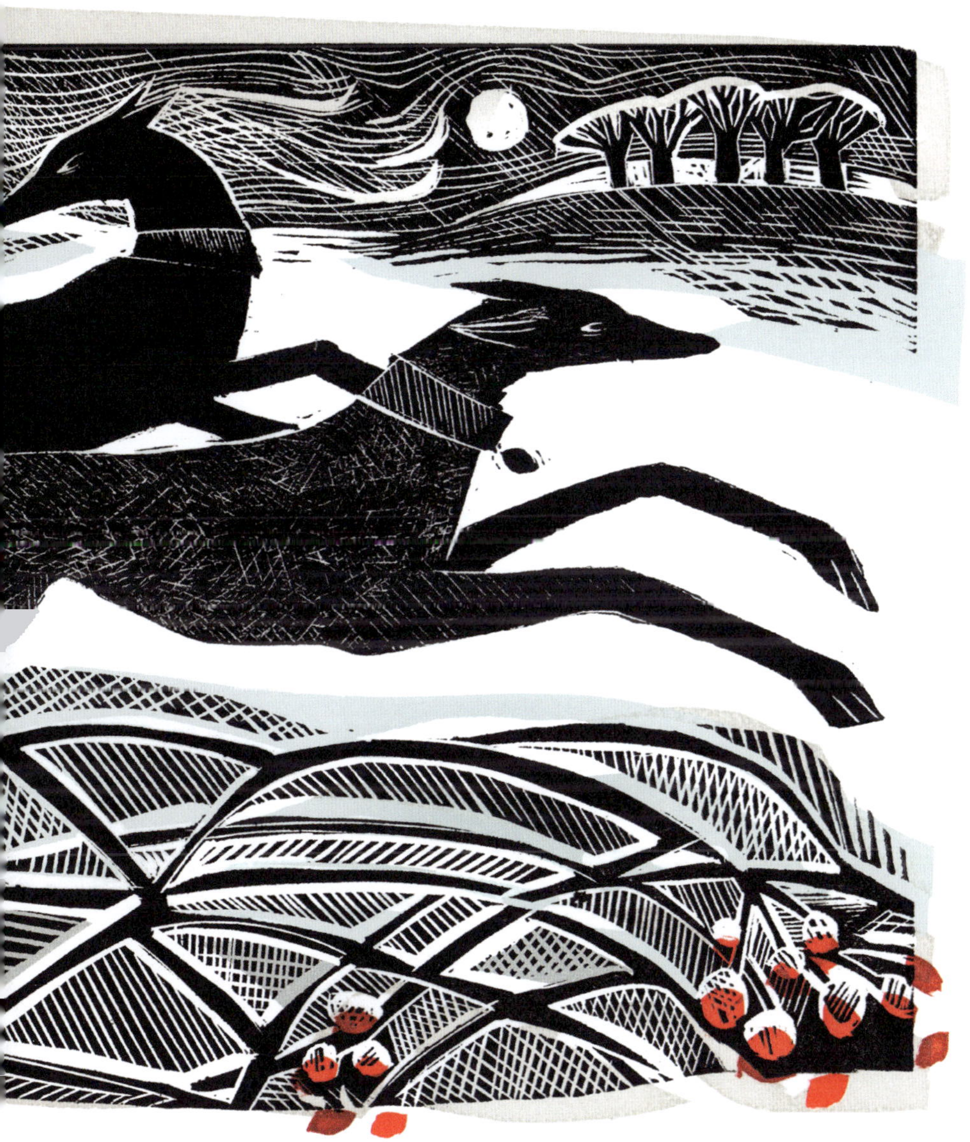

There are few more spectacular sights
than seeing the grey seals pupping
on the South Norfolk beaches of
Winterton and Horsey – a huge expanse
of beautiful sandy beach stretching out
as far as the eye could see and covered
with seals and their pups. But the
behaviour of many of the other visitors
was atrocious, truly shocking – putting
both themselves and the seal pups in
danger. The beaches are patrolled by
volunteers from a charity organisation,
Friends of Horsey Seals, but on the
day I visited there were just too many
people for them to control. It seemed
to highlight the great distance there
is between human understanding of
nature and how to respect it.

Opposite:
Seal Song
(Linocut and
silkscreen)

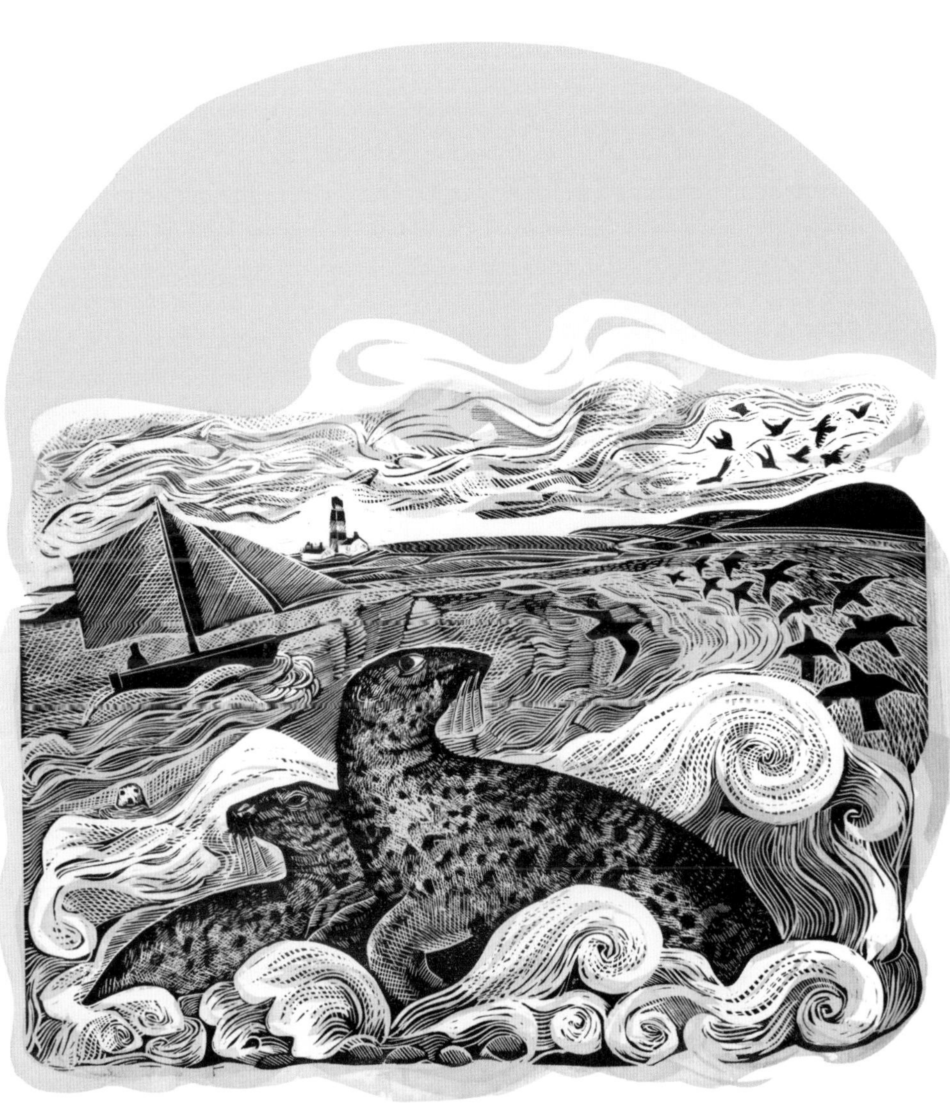

In the cold of winter, most squirrels
will be asleep, but when hunger stirs
them, you can see them scurry across
the ground with their tails nervously
flicking. Then they will stop and dig
to unearth the treasure trove of winter
food supplies that they buried in the
autumn. We have a walnut tree in
our garden and I am always amazed
by how the squirrels know that the
fruit is ready. Within days, they can
strip the tree bare, but I never mind,
as undoubtedly their need is greater
than mine.

Opposite:
Winter Squirrel
(Linocut and
silkscreen)

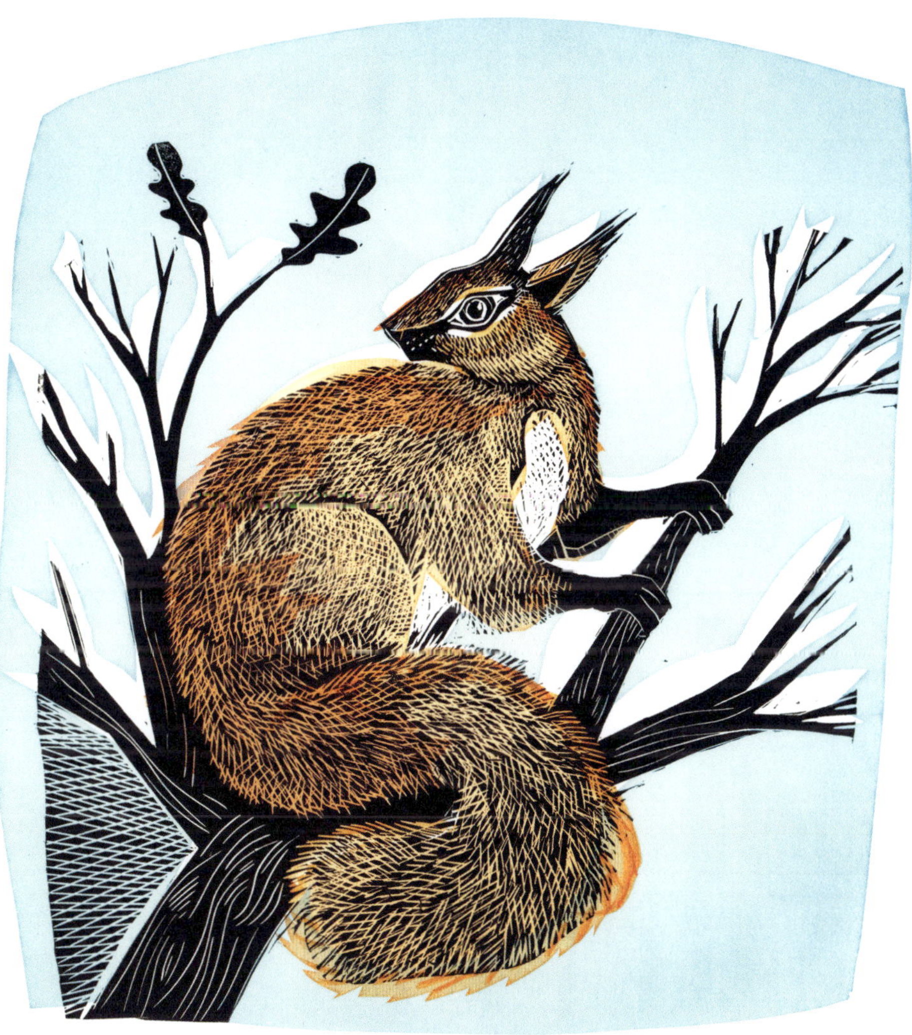

The arrival of the fieldfares and
redwings in Wing seems to bring the
year full circle. These birds migrate
from Scandinavia to overwinter in our
fields and woods. They are markers
that the days are growing shorter and
the nights darker. For Mark and me,
these winter days bring their own
cosiness. Every evening, we have the
ritual lighting of the wood burner; our
house is small, so the heat soon spreads
through the rooms. We are not the only
ones to enjoy a winter fire, as this is the
time when our whippets, Amy and Slim,
migrate full time to the sitting room –
ensuring they are the ones soaking up
the most heat.

Opposite:
Winter Walk
(Linocut and
silkscreen)

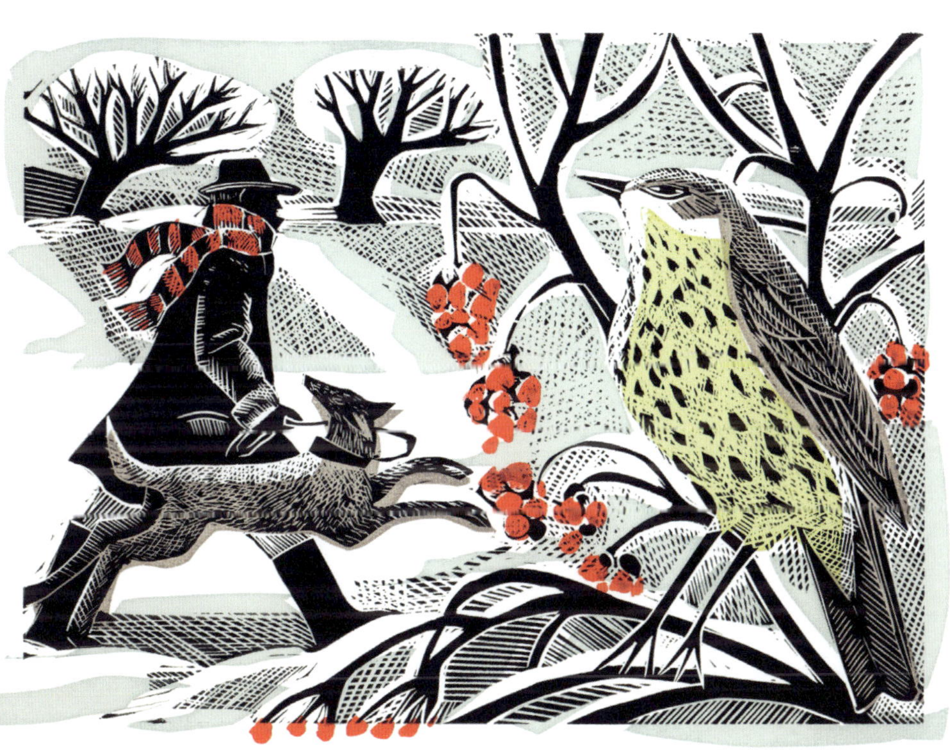

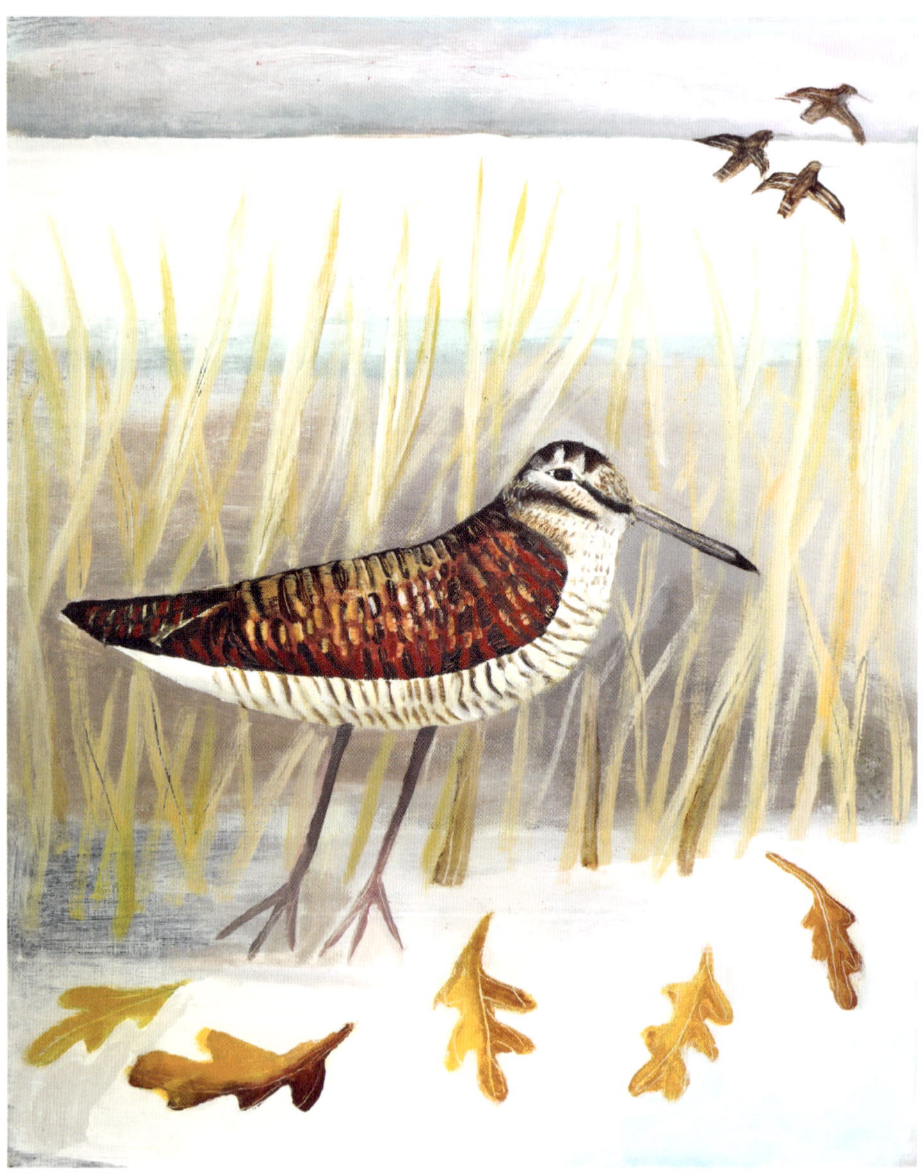

My friend Lyndon found a dead woodcock by Wing Lakes and brought it to my studio for me to draw and paint. Woodcocks are very hard to spot as they are mainly nocturnal and have extremely good camouflage. A bit bigger than a pigeon, with mottled brown, leaf-like plumage, they easily disappear into the background. Woodcocks come to the UK from Russia to overwinter, so it may have been that the poor bird had died of exhaustion. Its beautiful feathers were still in perfect condition, so it must not have been dead for long. The drawings I did of the bird that day became the reference material for the painting *Woodcock at the Frozen Lake*.

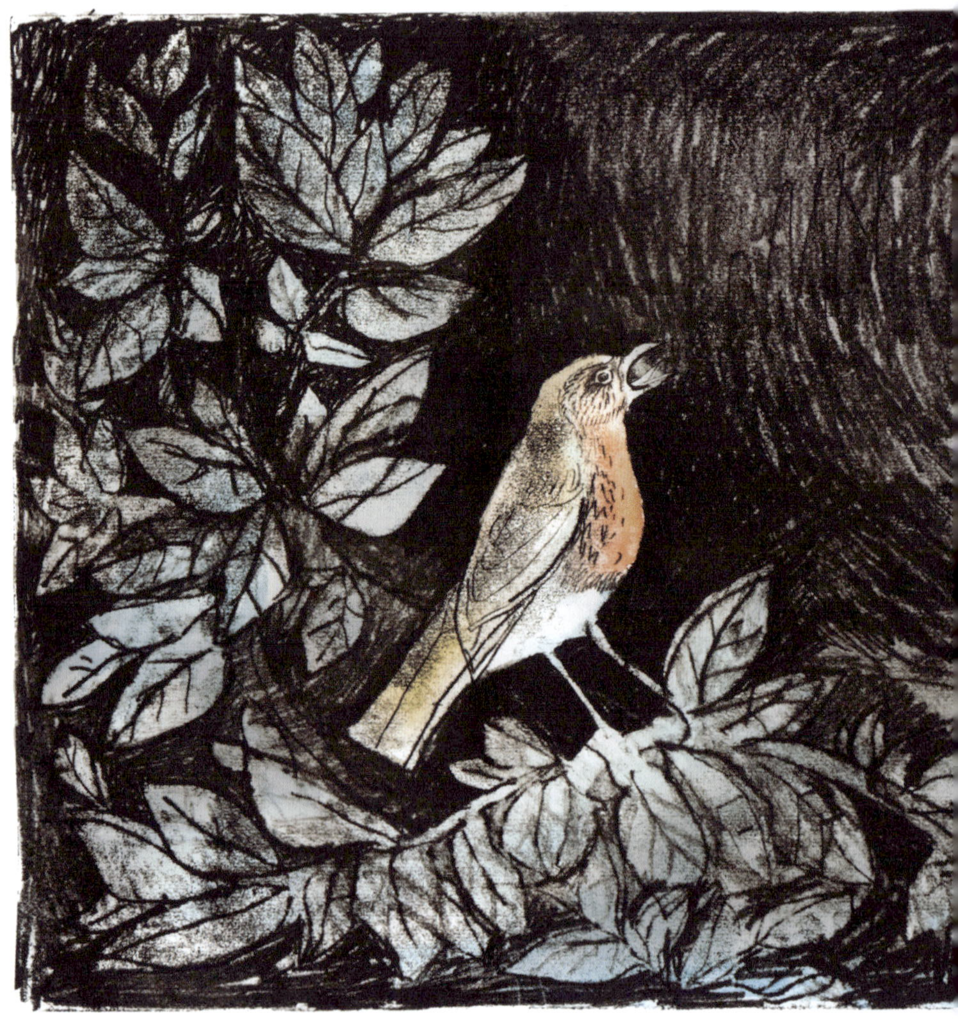

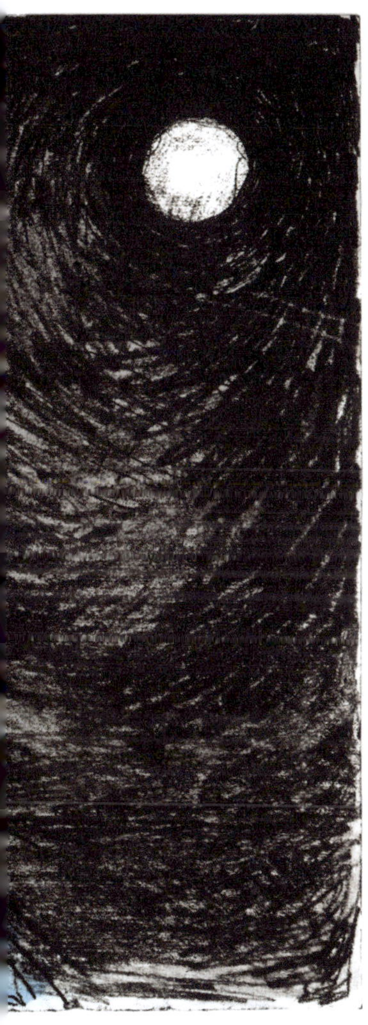

Robins are one of the few birds we have in the UK that sing throughout the year. They are very active little birds, using the whole of the day to feed, sing and defend their territories. It is quite common to hear them singing in the night. This is usually in towns and cities, where their singing is triggered by street lighting or other artificial lighting.

Opposite:
Night Singing Robins
(Monoprint)

It is always an incredible experience when you find yourself looking up on a clear night at a star-filled sky. It is on my to-do list to improve my ability to recognise star constellations. Orion's Belt, Ursa Major, also known as the Great Bear (the largest constellation in the northern hemisphere's sky), and the North Star are about my limit. There is definitely room for improvement.

Opposite:
Star Gazer
(Linocut and
silkscreen)

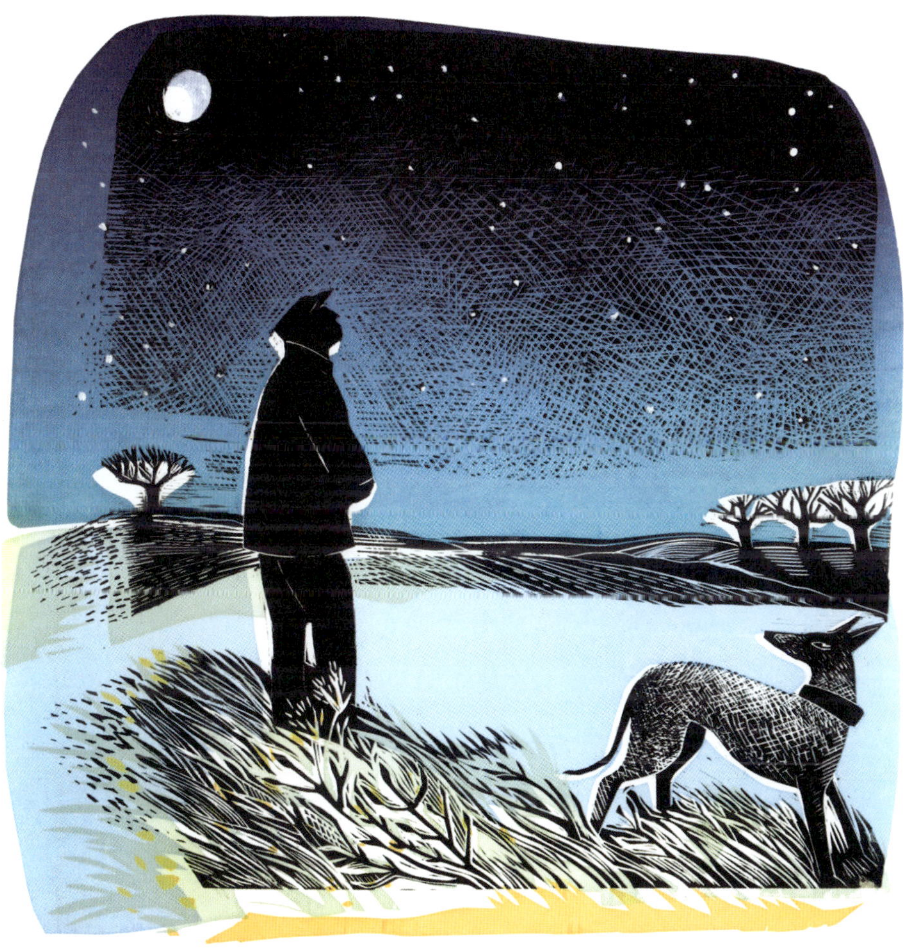

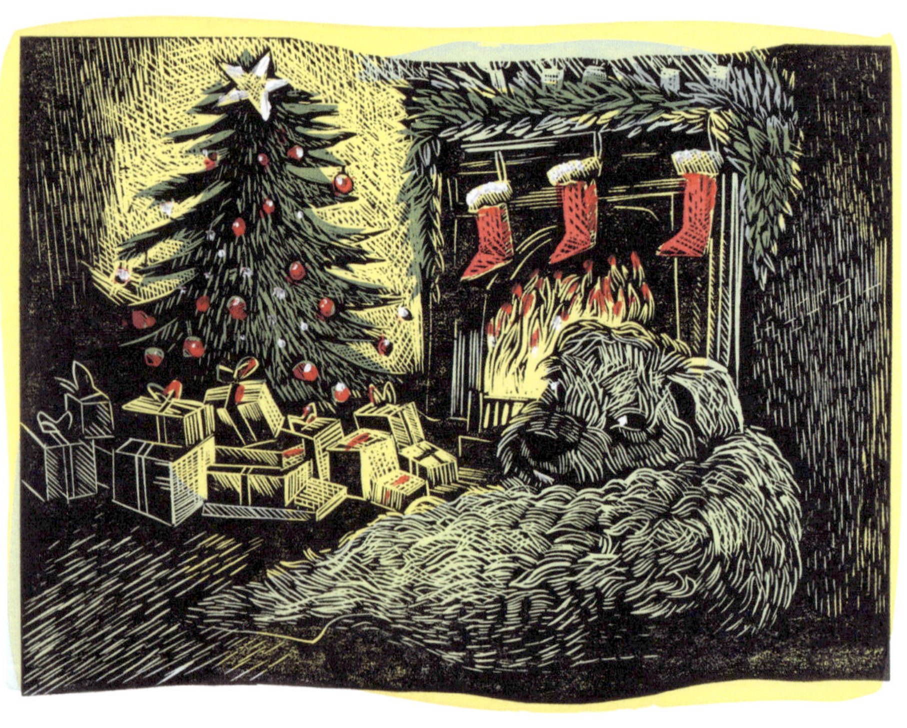

Though the illustration shown here is not a connection to nature, I am sure it is a connection to every household that has young children waiting for Christmas morning. Perhaps the truest expression of wakeful darkness is the small voice from upstairs calling, 'Is it morning yet?!'

The blue-green leaves of white glowing snowdrops pushing through the winter soil.

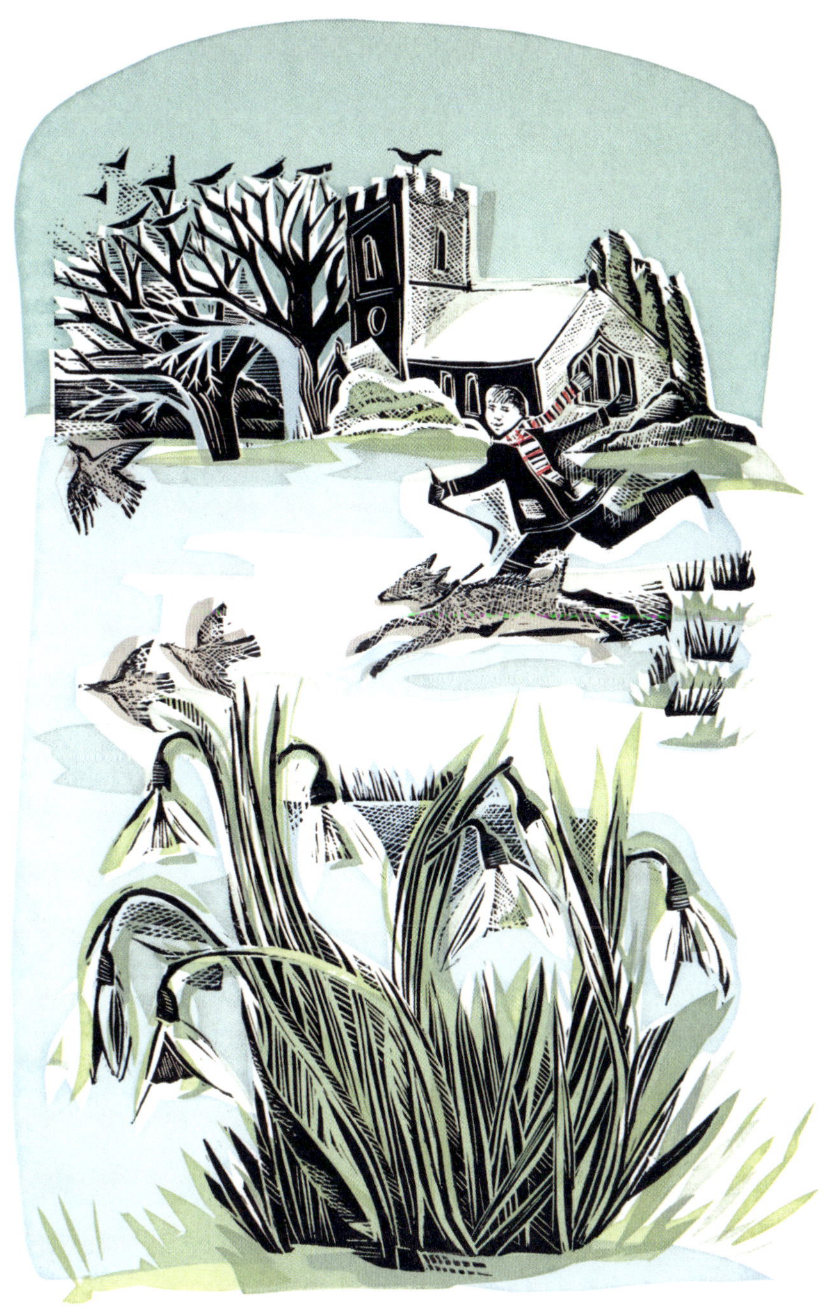

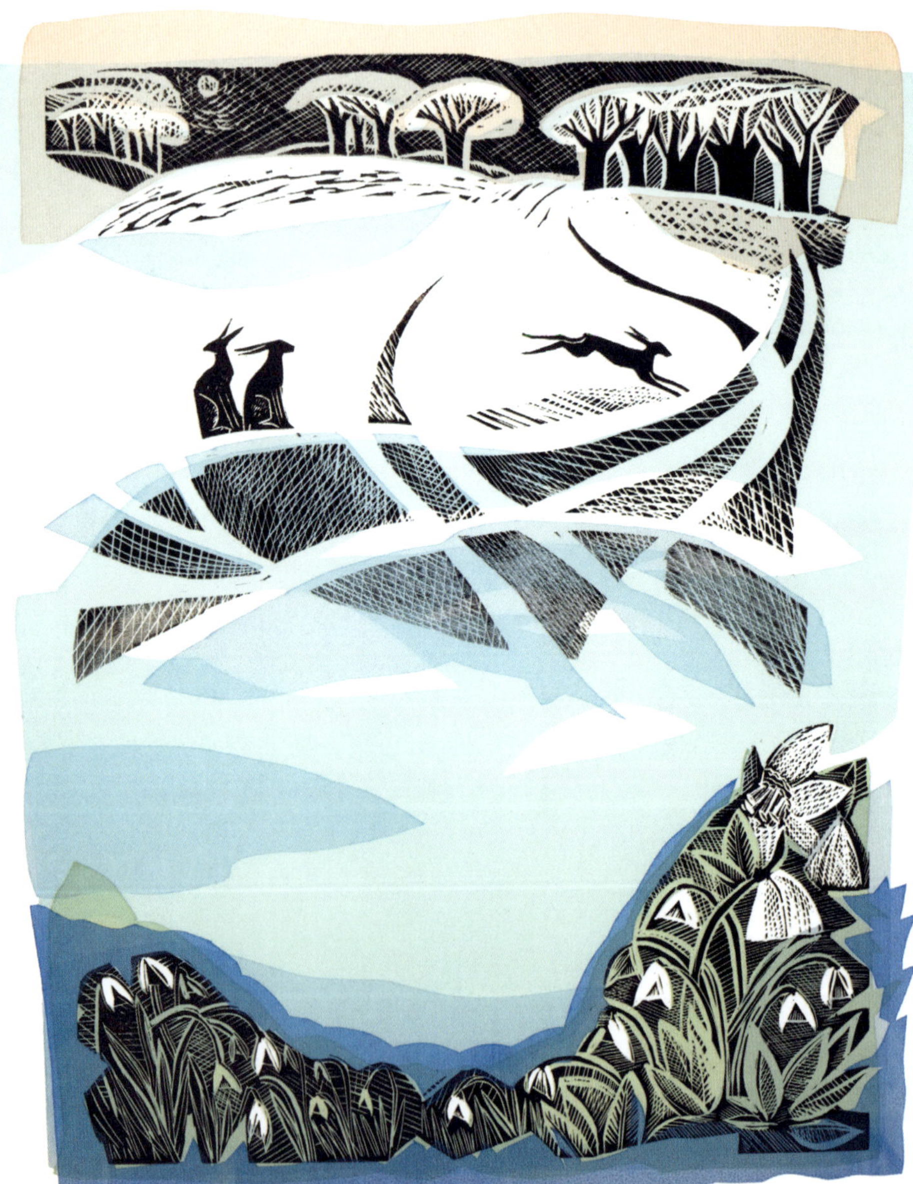

Winter weather is no excuse for not getting to work when your place of work is only a short walk down the garden path. I work most days and usually have a number of different projects on the go at the same time. This can be illustrations for book covers, calendars, cards, etc. Though I am often working on these projects from a set brief, the inspiration for the designs is always rooted in the things that I have seen. It is the changing seasons, the birds and animals that I observe on a daily basis that feed directly into my artwork. I consider myself very lucky to be able to express the joy I feel in nature and the things I see around me in the prints that I create. These illustrations are my attempt to portray a year unfolding.

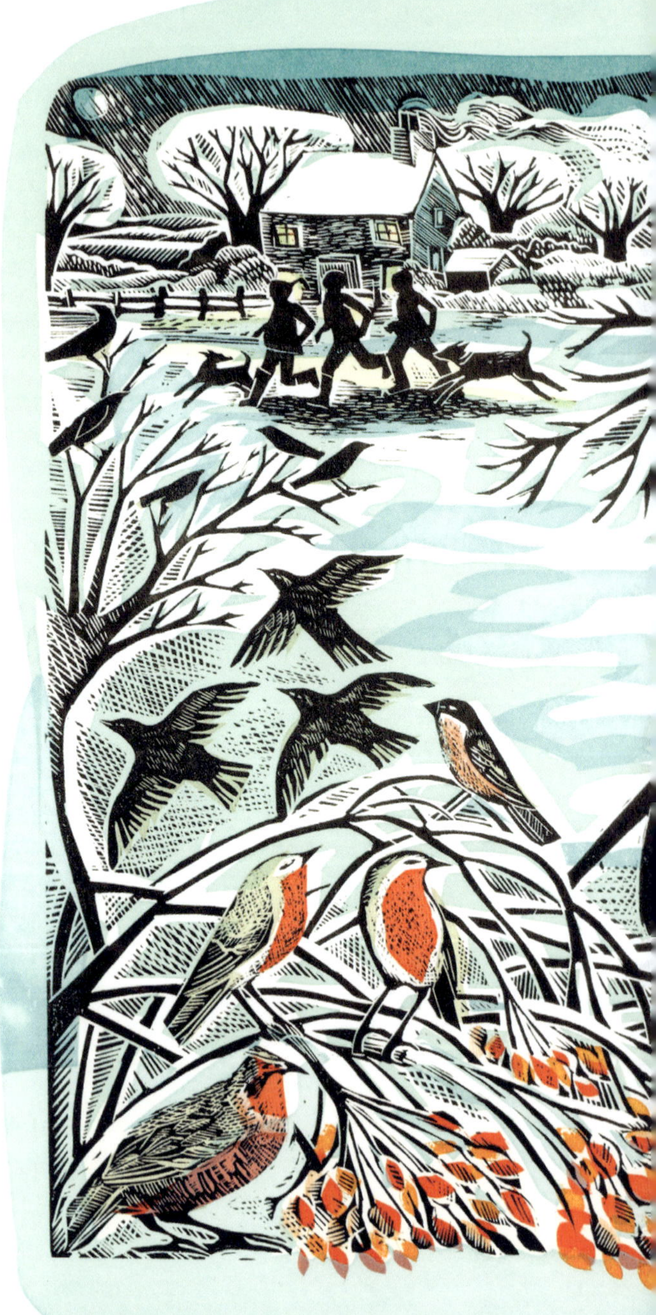

Right:
Winter Woodland
(Linocut and
silkscreen)

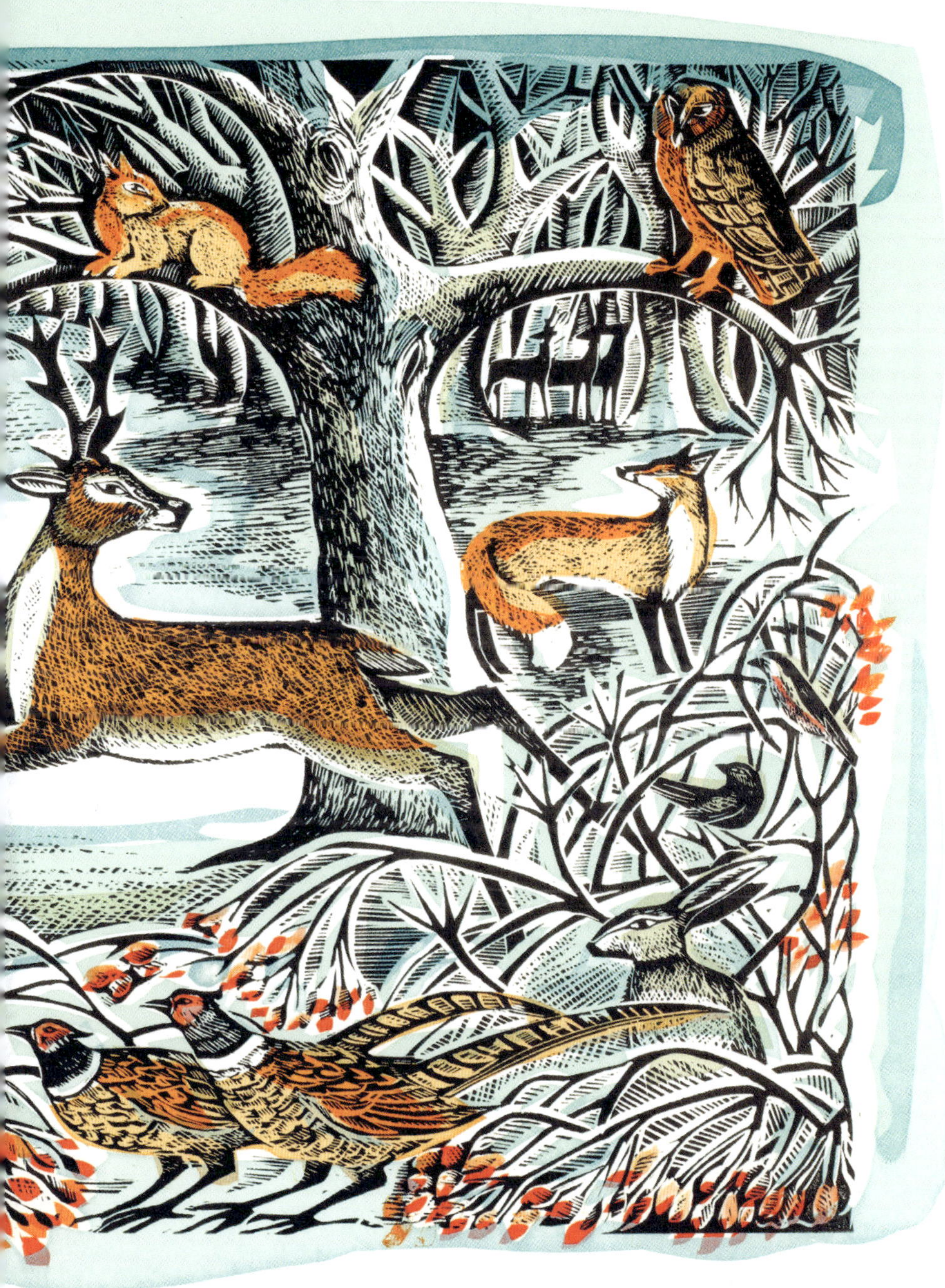

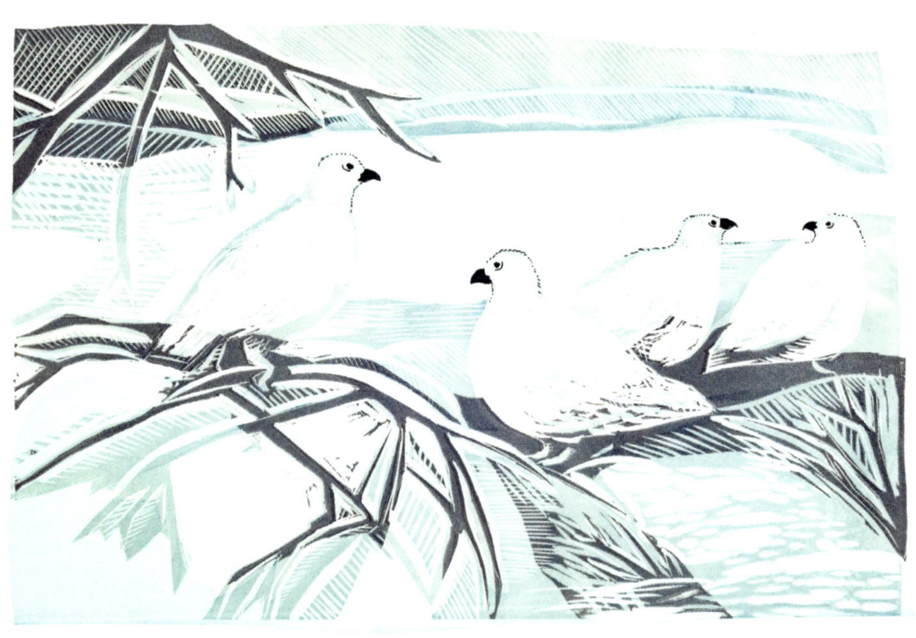

Ptarmigan can be found in the Highlands of Scotland where they live and breed. In the summer months, they are a mottled mix of browns and greys, but in winter they become completely white. This allows them to blend perfectly into their surroundings during both seasons.

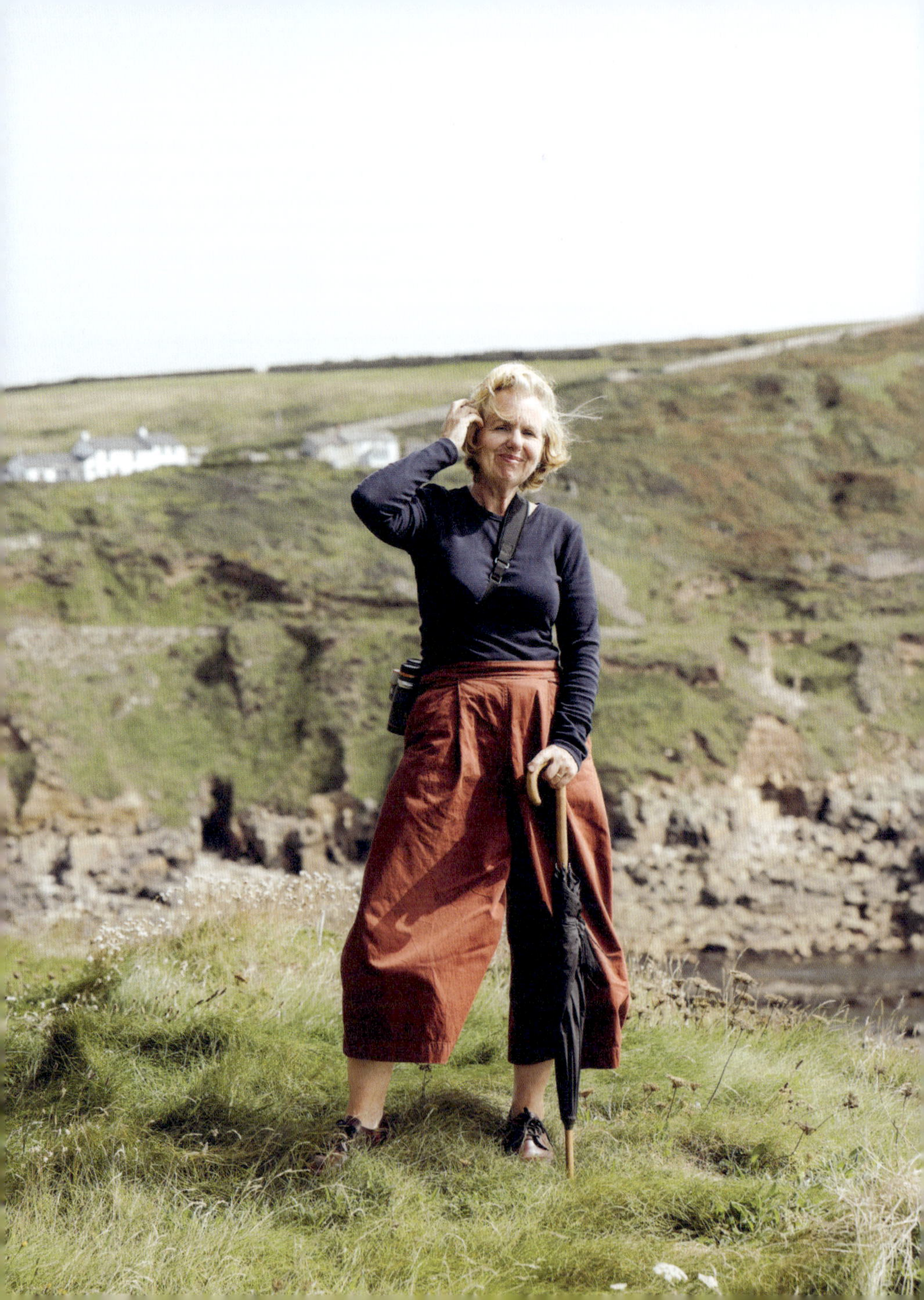

About the Author

ANGELA HARDING lives in the small county of Rutland and works out of the studio at the bottom of her garden in the village of Wing.

Angela has worked on the covers for a number of books, including P. D. James, Ted Hughes, Katya Balen and James Rebanks. Her children's book *RSPB Birds* by Miranda Krestovnikoff was longlisted for the Klaus Flugge prize. Her most recent children's book, *Wilding*, by Isabella Tree, was shortlisted for the 2024 Wainwright Prize for Children's Writing on Nature and Conservation. Other recent publications include *Blossomise* by Simon Armitage, a *Sunday Times* bestseller.

Angela has written and illustrated three books published by Little, Brown: *A Year Unfolding*, *Wild Light* and *Still Waters & Wild Waves*.

Angela's unique and distinct style has become instantly recognisable to nature lovers and book lovers alike. Her fans flock to buy her merchandise, including calendars, cards, tea towels, tote bags and jigsaws.

She was the 2024 artist for the 'Books Are My Bag' tote bag, celebrating independent bookshops across the UK and Ireland.

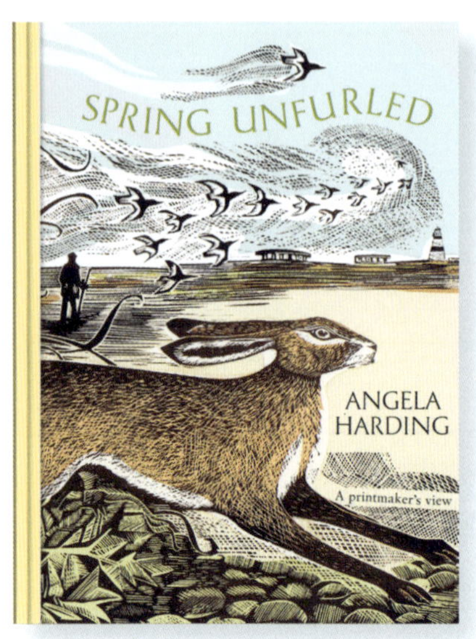

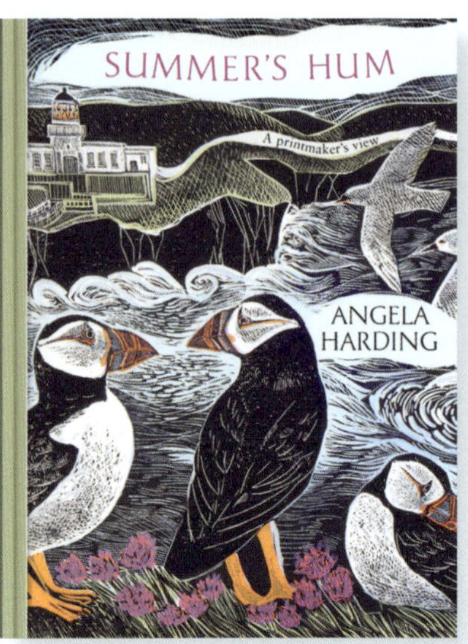

Collect the full Seasonal Quartet series

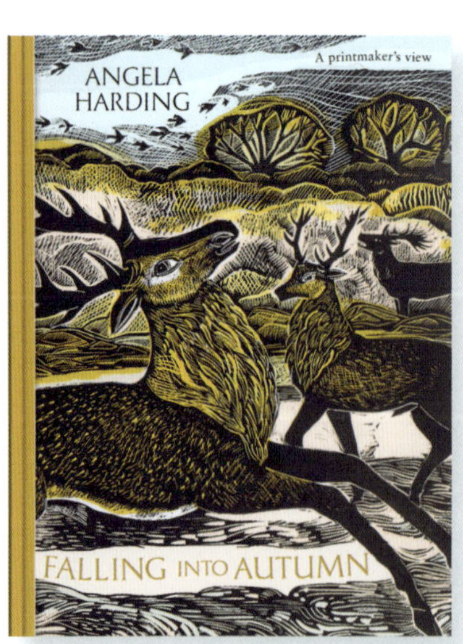

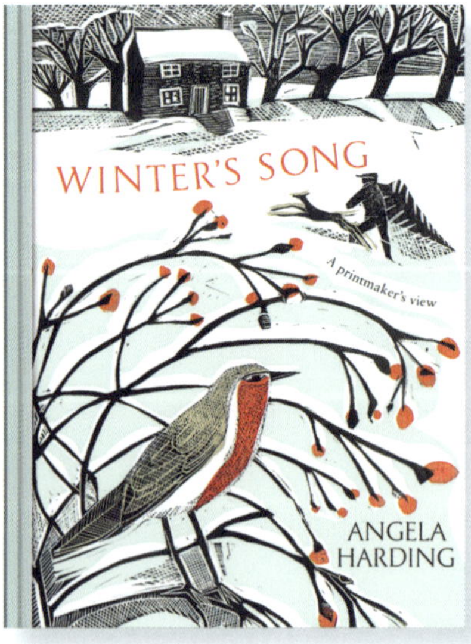

If you enjoyed *Winter's Song*, why not explore Angela's other books with Little, Brown

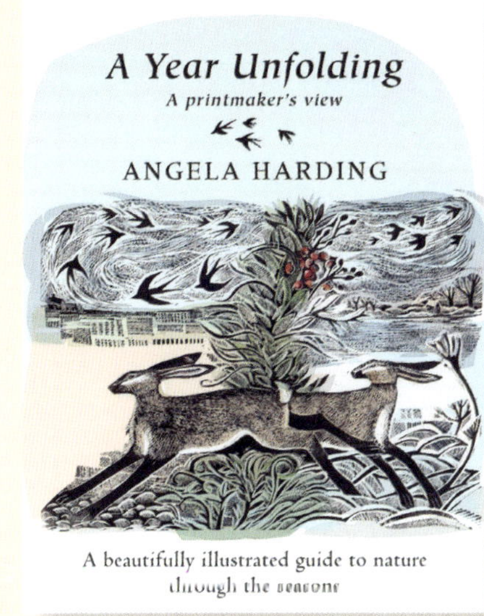

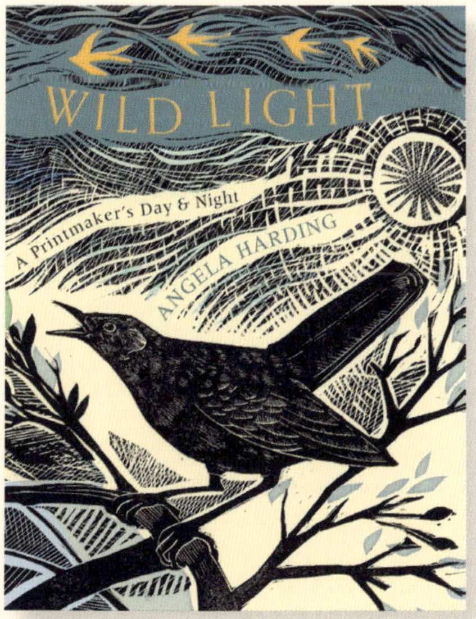

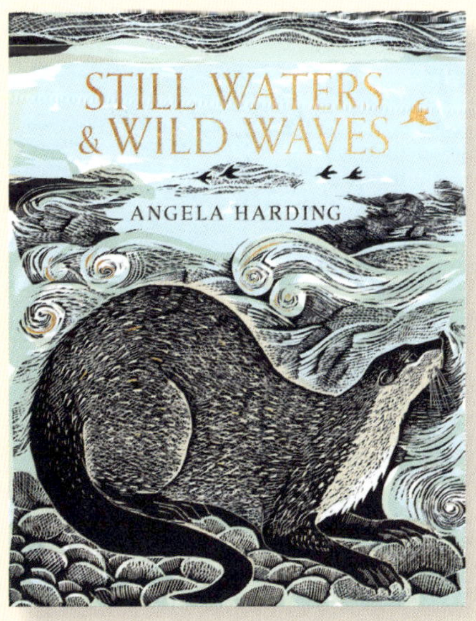

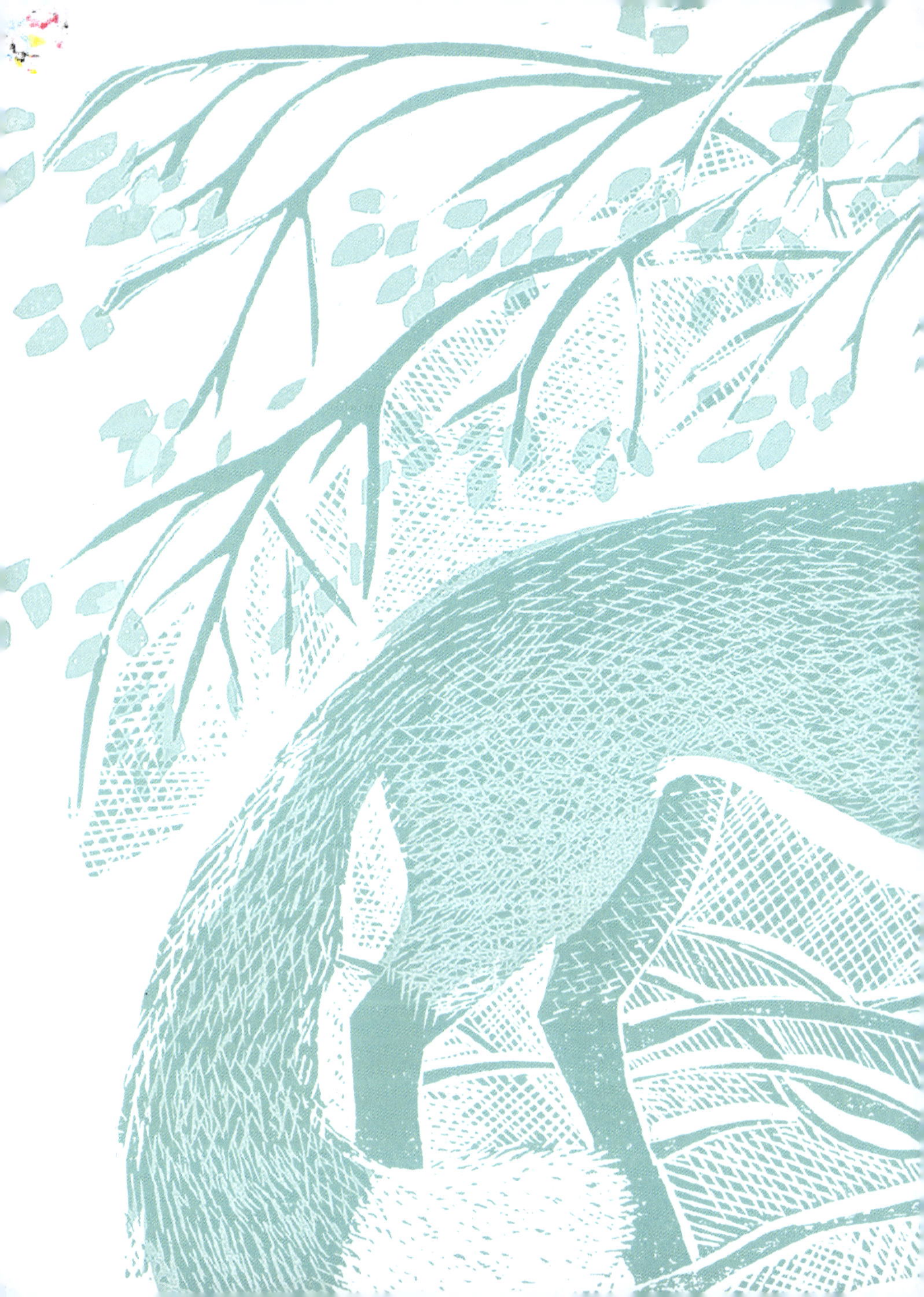